M000002616

One

Healing the Racial Divide

Dennis Rouse

One: Healing the Racial Divide
copyright ©2020 Dennis Rouse

ISBN: 978-1-950718-56-6

Printed in the United States of America

cover design by Joe Deleon

Avail
225 W. Seminole Blvd., Suite 105
Sanford, FL 32771

Unless otherwise noted, Scripture is from THE HOLY BIBLE, NEW INTERNATIONAL VERSION®, NIV® Copyright © 1973, 1978, 1984, 2011 by Biblica, Inc.® Used by permission. All rights reserved worldwide.

Scripture quotations marked MSG are taken from THE MESSAGE, copyright © 1993, 2002, 2018 by Eugene H. Peterson. Used by permission of NavPress. All rights reserved. Represented by Tyndale House Publishers, Inc.

Passages marked ESV are from The Holy Bible, English Standard Version. ESV® Text Edition: 2016. Copyright © 2001 by Crossway Bibles, a publishing ministry of Good News Publishers.

Passages marked NCV are taken from the New Century Version®. Copyright © 2005 by Thomas Nelson. Used by permission. All rights reserved.

Scripture quotations marked NLT are taken from the Holy Bible, New Living Translation, copyright © 1996, 2004, 2015 by Tyndale House Foundation. Used by permission of Tyndale House Publishers, Inc., Carol Stream, Illinois 60188. All rights reserved.

Passages marked NKJV are taken from the New King James Version®. Copyright © 1982 by Thomas Nelson. Used by permission. All rights reserved.

All rights reserved. No parts of this publication may be reproduced, stored in retrieval system or transmitted in any form or by any means—electronic, mechanical, photocopy, recording or otherwise—except for brief quotations in printed reviews, without the prior written permission of the author.

Contents

Foreword

I'VE KNOWN DENNIS and Colleen Rouse for over a decade, and walking alongside them in ministry has provided many of the most loving, rewarding and equipping experiences my wife Kristin and have ever had.

I'm currently 51 years young as I reflect and write this, and in my lifetime, I have had four spiritual dads and one spiritual father. I am grateful for these men and recognize the significance they all played in my life. The four spiritual dads happened to be black men, and they taught me most everything I needed to know about loving God, serving the church and using my musical gifts and talents to create religious experiences—mostly based in urban culture. Similar to the children of Israel, this shaped my first 40 years of life and religion. I didn't know it at the time, but I was stringing together emotional moments while looking for water in the desert.

However, the spiritual fathering would come from a white man, less than 10 years my senior. I'm intentionally making the distinction between dads and fathers for a reason; it only takes one time to be a dad, but fathering takes a life-time. Dennis Rouse has become that spiritual father figure, friend and faith walker for me to model. He showed me where the water was flowing in the dry places.

The history of race in America is why I point out that Dennis is white. My decade with Dennis developed my transition from religion to relationship (spiritually) and from toleration to reconciliation (naturally). He has been an integral part of my healing from some of the residual hurts I've personally experienced from our nation's history.

Without intentionality, our paths may have never crossed. Somehow, God intentionally orchestrated a harmonious meeting of an extremely white southern pastor and a famous, black R&B and hip-hop recording artist and created a symphony of beautiful years of doing life together. Together we have navigated de-escalating the ongoing racial tensions of our nation through the lens of the church without losing touch with the world. We have respectfully challenged each other regarding methods of providing diversity and inclusion in a multi-cultural, multi-generational church arena. We have loved each other and served together so that we could curate safe spaces for people of all nationalities to worship God as one. Dennis was intentional in showing me a "kingdom culture" kind of love that superseded personal preference, cultural expression and the desire to worship comfortably segregated.

I am a product of the teaching and mentorship of Dennis Rouse. My life in ministry and leadership would be unimaginable without his guidance and shared vision. I speak of the things we accomplished together because he has the ability to mobilize, encourage and empower the people around him to work together as one, as unto the Lord, to see things happen here on earth as they are in heaven.

I have been waiting for this book for quite some time. A few years ago, following Charlottesville, the world watched a viral video as an older white man repented, asked for forgiveness and washed the feet of a young black man. That was Dennis. What the world hasn't seen is how this man has done that same action daily to all the men and women around him, regardless of race or color. He lives it and breathes it and gets it, and now I'm glad he's finally written about it. Keep in mind, nobody gets it right every time; but ultimately, the goal is to get it.

As a man, specifically a Christian black man in America, I honor Dennis, not only as a husband, father and papa who loves his own family, but also as a man who loves all races equally and uniquely so that we may all have a little more heaven here on earth. There's no better time than right now for this book. We can all be uniquely who God created us to be, and still come together as one; Dennis is helping to show us the way.

—*Montell Jordan*
Grammy Nominated Recording Artist, Pastor, Author,
and co-founder of Marriage Masterpeace

chapter 1

Starting Point

*Our nation is desperate for healing ... and the
Church cannot be silent. Race was God's idea. Racial
reconciliation is at the heart of the gospel. —Rick Warren*

THE RAILROAD TRACKS running through the little Georgia town of McDonough were as much of a
dividing line as a brick wall would have been. The white
people lived on the north side, the blacks on the south.
When I grew up there in the 60s, there were very few, if
any, Hispanics or Asians, but race was the hottest topic on
every level, from the federal government to conversations
with friends. The Civil Rights Act passed in 1964 and the
Voting Rights Act a year later. Attempts to desegregate
the country focused on schools. Congress mandated better educational opportunities for black children, and the
state's solution was to bus kids from one part of town to the
other. When I entered the eighth grade, I was selected to

attend previously all-black Westside High School (which started with my grade and went through the twelfth).

Getting there every day proved to be an ordeal. I had to take a bus from my home to the railroad tracks and transfer to another bus for the second leg to school. On the first day when I walked into my homeroom, it was starkly apparent that for the first time in my life, I was in the minority. Only a handful of kids looked like me.

It was a difficult year for me. For the first time in my life, I was a member of a minority! Black boys picked on me and called me names, and I got into a lot of fights. I wasn't the only one who had trouble fitting in. All year, the tension built. Prejudice on both sides took the form of wordless sneers, name-calling, all kinds of other verbal offenses, and fights. Near the end of the year, the pent-up anger exploded into a full-scale riot that made national news!

The match that lit the fuse was anger over student-government elections. Since the school was predominantly black, black candidates won every seat in every grade. The principal wanted at least the appearance of balance, so he unilaterally chose a white kid to be vice president of the student council. What started off as a protest outside the school soon turned into something much bigger. Cars were turned over and set on fire, and fights broke out between black and white students. Eventually the police arrived to try and calm things down, but the damage was already done. From that moment, many white families pulled their children out of public schools and started private schools across the state of Georgia, with many of them initially meeting in churches and using the term "Christian" to describe their schools.

That year, the Baptist church where our family attended started a private school, and from that time, I never went to school with black students again. In this sequestered environment, I wasn't forced to think very deeply about prejudice. It would be years later that I really considered the issue of racism in America.

After graduating from high school, I attended the University of Georgia. At the time, very few students were black, Hispanic, or Asian. My fraternity brothers were all white, my friends were all white, and almost everybody in my classes was white.

Five years later, after finishing my time at Georgia, I moved to New Jersey to start a business. About six months into the founding of the business, I had an encounter with God that changed my life forever. While I didn't go to church at the time, I did begin reading the Bible. The more I read, the more I began to realize that I had never really understood the message of Jesus—and how He values everyone—regardless of race or culture. Eventually, I met my wife Colleen, and we both felt God leading us to move to Richmond, Virginia, to help with a small church plant. At the time, it was an all-white congregation of about 50 people, but that was about to change!

A Surprise for All of Us

Colleen and I wanted to do something to make people who were new to the church feel welcome, so every Sunday, we would invite an individual or a family to have lunch with us at my small apartment. One Sunday morning, a young black woman came to church and sat down with her three little girls, about two, four, and six years old. After the service, Colleen and I introduced ourselves. The woman replied, "I'm Delise. It's nice to meet you." When we invited them to my home for lunch, she looked very surprised. She responded, "Well, yes, we'd love to." I gave her directions, and a few minutes later, she and her daughters were sitting with us at a card table (which served as my dining table) as Colleen served lunch.

I said, "Let me thank the Lord for our food." As I started to pray, Delise began to cry. Immediately, I stopped and asked, "What's wrong?"

Through her tears and as her little girls stared at her, she said, "I'm just overwhelmed. This is the first time I've ever been invited into a white person's house. I've been a maid for white people, but in my life, I've never been asked to sit at a table with them."

At that moment, I had the stark realization that I had absolutely no comprehension of the pain she felt in a prejudiced society that put black people in a subservient place. I didn't have a clue what they faced. Her heart was melted by our simple invitation, and my heart was broken by the profound sadness she continually experienced. I was determined to do something about it, but I had no idea what steps I could take.

When Delise and the girls left after lunch, Colleen and I sat down for a heart-to-heart conversation about what had just happened. We couldn't fix the racial divide in America, but we could do some things to be sure Delise and her daughters felt welcome and loved at our church—and in our lives. In other words, we weren't willing for the lunch to be a one-off experience for them or for us.

I guess our lunch was enough of an affirmation for Delise and the girls to come back to church the next week, and the next, and after a while, Delise joined the worship team. On her first Sunday helping to lead worship, she blew us away. We had no idea she could play the piano so well and sing so beautifully. Within weeks, more black people started attending our little church, and without any planning at all, we became a multicultural body.

Occasionally, Colleen and I did some babysitting for Delise, and we became very close to the whole family. When we got married a few months later, the middle daughter, Andrea, was the flower girl at our wedding.

"The rest of the story" is that Delise eventually married a white man in the church, and they moved to Nashville to pursue a music career with the children. A few years later, the three daughters formed a popular Christian group called Out of Eden and recorded several albums that blessed many.

Having Delise and the girls over for lunch was a turning point in our lives. From that day forward, Colleen and I began to develop friendships with any black and brown people who started coming to the church. We were in a small group led by a black couple, Pete and Minnie Edmonds, who became mentors to us. Years before, I'd avoided getting near black people, but now my wife and I were submitting ourselves to black people in leadership. This became a huge turning point in the church: For the first time, whites were following and submitting to black leadership—something we had never seen before!

A Different Kind of Church

Seven years later, in 1990, after graduating from Bible college, we moved back to my home state of Georgia and started a church in Norcross, an Atlanta suburb. As we launched our church, I asked God for a clear vision of what He wanted to accomplish in us and through us, and He pointed me to a passage in the book of Acts where Luke records the final words of Jesus before He ascended to heaven: "But you will receive power when the Holy Spirit comes upon you. And you will be my witnesses, telling people about me everywhere—in Jerusalem, throughout Judea, in Samaria, and to the ends of the earth" (Acts 1:8, NLT). As I began to meditate on that verse, I felt like God was saying that we were to build the church on four pillars that would be the foundation of our vision: Jerusalem represented the concept of "building strong families," Judea represented "transforming our community," Samaria represented "reconciling cultures," and the ends of the earth represented "world missions." I was amazed—I had never noticed that Jesus included the concept of cultural reconciliation in the Great Commission, but it was right there all along. As I studied the background of Jesus' commission to the church, I discovered the Samaritans were the archenemies of the Jews. The two groups were suspicious of each other, felt superior to each other, and wanted to avoid each other. It was very similar to the tension we see between different races in our country today.

In the first century, Samaria wasn't just a spot on a map that was no different from the surrounding areas. When Jewish people spoke of Samaria, their words were filled with disgust and hate. The Samaritans were considered half-breeds, the descendants of Jews left behind during the Assyrian captivity centuries earlier and Assyrians who occupied their land. The Jews hated them. In fact, when they traveled between Galilee and Jerusalem, many of them took a much longer circuitous route to avoid going through Samaria. But Jesus didn't take the long route. On one of his trips, He met "the woman at the well." She was especially despised by the Jews because she was a Samaritan, a woman, and an adulteress—three strikes, and you're out! But in His last charge to the disciples, Jesus told them specifically to go to Samaria, to care for the Samaritans, and to make them part of the new church ... because God loved them. I can imagine the disciples looking at each other and whispering, "Are you kidding? Anyone but them!" But Jesus made it clear that He wanted them to go where others refused to go.

Jesus' vision of the church was a place where every person—regardless of race, culture, or history—would be welcome. It was to be a place where people could be forgiven from their pasts and start living out their futures with God's love as the guiding force. He knew this would be difficult because history was littered with conflict between cultures, but He explained that when people truly believe in Him and are willing to submit to Him, their hearts are transformed. Their lives enter a new dimension of love they never knew existed. Cultural reconciliation can only happen when people are transformed by the love of God. This is hard for people to understand if they haven't been transformed from the inside out by God's grace. If our hearts haven't been changed so that we love those we used to avoid, we'll continue to live with suspicious minds, wounded hearts, and entrenched habits that keep us separated.

As I kept reading Luke's account in the book of Acts, I realized the church was multicultural from the very beginning. On Passover, when 120 of Jesus' followers gathered in an upper room to pray, God had brought all the nations of the world to Jerusalem. While the disciples prayed, suddenly they started speaking in languages that represented all the people gathered in the streets. It was a supernatural phenomenon that captured the attention of people from all the nations. That day, three thousand of them believed in Jesus and became the first members of the New Testament church. That's right—the first Christians created a multicultural, multigenerational church that turned the world upside down! It's still hard for me to wrap my head around what that must have looked like as the different cultures began gathering in each other's homes, spending time with each other's families, and breaking bread together. From the first days, the church was the place where racial and cultural reconciliation would be modeled for the world to see.

The story of Jesus changing lives began by His welcoming people from all cultures, and it will end that way. John's Revelation can be a scary (and intriguing) part of the Bible, but we need to pay attention to what our ultimate destiny will look like. John gives us a glimpse of the future: "After this I looked, and behold, a great multitude that no one could number, from every nation, from all tribes and peoples and languages, standing before the throne and before the Lamb, clothed in white robes, with palm branches in their hands" (Revelation 7:9, ESV).

Our church was founded on the belief that what happened in Jerusalem that day should happen today in our church and in churches throughout the world. Bringing races together with the glue of God's love shouldn't be odd or new or unusual in any way. It should be entirely normal.

But the question still remains: Is it normal? Do people of color feel completely accepted and comfortable when they walk into a church filled with white people? Do white people feel loved and accepted when they walk into a church dominated by another race? If not, could it be that our racial preferences are more important to us than the kingdom of God?

The love of God—the real thing, not just lip service—bridges racial divides and helps us identify with those who don't look like us, don't talk like us, don't think like us, and don't eat like us. When our church started, I was so sure this was a priority in the heart of God that I set a goal of having 100 nationalities represented at Victory. Today, we have people from 142 countries who are involved in the life of our church. When I look at our crowd, I get a glimpse of what Peter saw as he spoke in Jerusalem on that pivotal day in history, and I get a taste of what it will be like to stand before the throne with the multitude of brothers and sisters from all over the world.

The motto of our country is *e pluribus unum*: out of many, one. And it's what God wants for all who believe in Him. Out of many nations, out of many backgrounds, out of many political persuasions, God welds us into one.

Two Cultures

Two cultures exist in every church, and the one that has the ascendancy is the one the church is known for—especially by people of different races. The *earthly culture* is a reflection of the goals of people throughout the community. It seeks power, wants to dominate, craves attention, cares only for its own kind, and therefore, divides people by race, class, gender, and age. The *kingdom culture* is the polar opposite. It gives away power: Jesus said that if you want to be great, you'll have to become the servant of all. It's upside down: the last shall be first and the first last. It doesn't depend on intelligence, the urge to dominate, or the power of money; instead, it values kindness, compassion, and justice for the oppressed. A kingdom culture unites people around their common experience of the matchless grace of God.

Most churches talk about the kingdom of God, but their DNA is that of the earthly culture. When we walk through their doors, we see homogeneous congregations, not the wide diversity they saw in Jerusalem and we'll see at the end of time. Certainly, sameness eliminates tension and makes people comfortable, but it also eliminates opportunities to shine like lights of love to a broken and discouraged world.

White people, let me ask you: When black and brown people come to your church, do they come back? Do they bring their friends because they feel so welcomed?

And black and brown people, let me ask you: When white people come to your church, do they come back? Do they bring their friends because they feel loved?

In the kingdom, being comfortable isn't the highest goal. Jesus gave himself for people who are nothing like Him. How comfortable was the ridicule, the scourging, the crown of thorns, and the cross? In an abundance of love for those who aren't like Him—you and me—He became incredibly uncomfortable. The willingness to suffer for others—or at least to be uncomfortable as we demonstrate our love for them—is a sign of His kingdom.

Does it take work for church leaders to create a kingdom culture? Absolutely. We have to be aware of our words, illustrations, and song selections. We must consider how the faces of the people on the stage and every other aspect of church life relates to people of all races and classes. For instance, when I speak about God's plan for the family, I don't make the assumption that everyone in the audience is from a white, intact, middle to upper-income household. I know I'm speaking to a much wider range of family situations, so I make sure to include several illustrations and applications.

Does it take courage for individuals to live out a kingdom culture? Of course. It's safer and easier to spend time with people like us, but it takes work to understand people who are different. What are their dreams? What do they dread? How do they relate to issues in the news? Do we know? Will we listen? Do we even care?

Highs and Lows

As we've tried to create a kingdom culture in our church, we've had plenty of highs and lows. One of the things I've noticed over the years of pastoring a multicultural church is how different races view the concept of reconciliation. People of color have had to adapt to a white-majority world. When they visit our church, they're very happy that they are finally being welcomed into a church that values them as much as anyone else. Many people of color who were suspicious of white people in authority have decided to work through some of their wounds from the past and try to overcome their trust issues. They want to be part of this beautiful story of reconciliation. Many blacks, Hispanics, and Asians have said, "Wow, I didn't know there was a place where white people actually want us!"

I've seen that when people of color go to a church led by a white pastor and they feel loved, it can be a deeply healing experience. They believe they gain something from being there. But when white people attend a church led by a black pastor, they believe they lose something of themselves—their traditions, their comfort, their identities—by being there. White people are used to being in power, on top, and in control, so when they're not, it feels very awkward. For this reason, it can sometimes be more challenging for whites to participate in a multicultural church than for people of color.

Over the years, I've been thrilled to see people's eyes light up when I talk about a kingdom culture and call people to love those who are different from them, but I've been disheartened by two things: the apathy of many in the white community and the anger that sometimes overwhelms the black and brown communities. I'm quite sure there are plenty of angry whites, but they don't usually come to our church, and there may be apathetic blacks, but in my view, that's more of an expression of depression than apathy. Over the years, it's been very difficult to watch many of my white friends and white pastors bail out when tension begins to rise. I've seen far too many people more interested in protecting themselves than being willing to get involved in the fray. Some white pastors have told me, "If I say too much or get too involved in issues of racial reconciliation, people will leave my church, and I'll lose many of my friends." On the other side, I've also heard the frustration and anger from blacks about the slow pace of change and the lack of white voices calling for systematic racism to end. A few black leaders have told me that they're done trying to work with white people, and they're just going to focus on healing their own communities.

All of this only perpetuates the problem. Leaders who abdicate their responsibility to be agents of reconciliation leave a void in society that eventually polarizes into what we see today. Fringe groups step into the void and create environments of fear and intimidation, which only serve to make the problem worse. To complicate matters, we see videos on social media and the news that magnify the fringe groups' actions, which cause people who are watching to become fearful of what's coming next! At this crucial moment, the church must not stay silent. The world is looking for leadership.

In one-race churches, it's easy to find people who agree with you about gun violence, the cure for poverty, immigration, healthcare, and a host of other issues. But in a multicultural church, the person sitting next to you may have very different views. Proximity forces us to stop, engage, listen, and try to understand the other side of every argument. As we've dealt with national problems of political upheaval, riots, murders, and lame excuses, the vast majority of people in our church have had the guts to stay and work things through. I admire their tenacity and their love for others in the church.

Responses Outside the Church

A few years ago, I was invited to speak to a group of local government officials in the county where our church is located. For a number of years, the county had been going through a major demographic change, and it had become the second most multicultural county in the United States. The area had been predominately white for many years, but it was experiencing what many call "white flight" as white families began to move north and west into communities that weren't integrated to any significant extent. The county officials faced a challenge because most of the governing authorities were still white. The leaders wanted me to share our church's experience of learning how to adjust to the new environment.

After I shared from a biblical perspective what would be necessary to help people get along and grow together, it became apparent that there were two different views on what I'd said. After finishing my talk, the few black and brown officials that were there were the first to come up and shake my hand and thank me. I think it was the first time the county officials had ever addressed the issue in this format. But I also noticed that the white leaders seemed to struggle with my message. When I finished, they walked out of the room without a word. It was a classic response to the power struggle we see playing out every day in America. Later, a few of the white leaders called me to say they were sympathetic to my message, but they didn't feel at liberty to share their views with their friends watching. Today, the county has a black commissioner for the first time in history, and I'm finally seeing some progress. The lesson I learned is that sometimes you have to be willing to speak the truth in love and allow God to do the work that only He can do in the hearts of people.

Sometimes it doesn't look like any progress is being made, but God is working behind the scenes doing things no person can do. In my experience, the love of Jesus is the only thing that can ultimately change how people think and act.

People often try to put me in a box: left or right, Democrat or Republican. In this book, I'm not suggesting just a blend of the two political views. I'm offering a third vantage point, nothing watered down, nothing compromised, but based on firm convictions that a kingdom culture values personal responsibility *and* compassion for everyone—especially for those who've been devalued in society. Don't be hesitant to push back on my ideas. The crucible of give-and-take is where we learn and grow.

At the end of each chapter, you'll find some questions. These are designed for personal reflection and group discussion. The goal isn't to rush through them. I hope you'll take plenty of time to use these questions to consider what you've read.

Think About It:

What is your experience, positive and painful, with people of other races and cultures?

Who do you know whose love for people of other races is most like Jesus' love for people who are so different from Him? Does that person inspire you, confuse you, or infuriate you? Explain your answer.

To what extent have your experiences created an earthly culture in your family and among your friends? To what extent have they created a kingdom culture?

Is the love of Jesus so real to you that it overwhelms your natural, normal, racial prejudice? Explain your answer.

What do you hope to get out of this book?

chapter 2

"It's Not Fair!"

*A loving person lives in a loving world. A hostile person
lives in a hostile world. Everyone you meet is your mirror.*
—Ken Keyes, Jr.

A FEW DECADES AGO, people who differed on social policies could be friends who enjoyed spending time with each other. In the 1980s, Democratic House
Majority Leader Tip O'Neill often went to the White
House to enjoy a relaxed time of friendship with Republican President Ronald Reagan. Today, we find very few
friendships among people who are on opposite sides of
the political and social divide. In a *New York Times* opinion piece, journalist Thomas Edsall observes,

> Hostility to the opposition party and its candidates has
> now reached a level where loathing motivates voters
> more than loyalty. ... The building strength of parti-
> san antipathy—"negative partisanship"—has radically

altered politics. Anger has become the primary tool for motivating voters.[1]

In a Fox News editorial, Salena Zito comments,

The vitriol of Washington politics has certainly escalated since the late 1990s, when it was granted a big stage on cable TV with a nonstop news cycle. In the last 10 years, the rise of social media has fueled even more mocking and destruction.[2]

It's not that we disagree about immigration, DACA (Deferred Action for Childhood Arrivals), healthcare, tax policy, troop withdrawals, and a host of other issues. It's that we believe people who disagree with us are fools.

Class War

Sociologist Arlie Russell Hochschild wanted to study the paradox that many people, especially white people, who need government assistance are strongly opposed to it. She studied a group of people in Louisiana and found its complaints rooted in three factors: flat or falling wages,

---

1. "What Motivates Voters More than Loyalty? Loathing," Thomas Edsall, *New York Times*, March 1, 2018, https://www.nytimes.com/2018/03/01/opinion/negative-partisanship-democrats-republicans.html

2. "Salena Zito: Elites are the ones who are dividing America," Salena Zito, Fox News, October 7, 2018, https://www.foxnews.com/opinion/salena-zito-elites-are-the-ones-who-are-dividing-america

rapid demographic changes, and liberal elites who mock their faith in God and their loyalty to American ideals. A particular phrase became the title of her book: *Strangers in Their Own Land*. Two other phrases form her conclusions: "cutting in line" and "the deep story."

When Barack Obama was elected President, many believed America was on the verge of a breakthrough in race relations. Hochschild found just the opposite. As she listened to people she interviewed, she came up with an analogy to describe their perspective, one they considered completely wrong and unfair. She peppered her explanation with their words:

> "You are patiently standing in a long line" for something you call the American dream. You are white, Christian, of modest means, and getting along in years. You are male. There are people of color behind you, and "in principle you wish them well." But you've waited long, worked hard, "and the line is barely moving."

> Then "Look! You see people cutting in line ahead of you! You're following the rules. They aren't. As they cut in, it feels like you are being moved back. How can they just do that?" Who are these interlopers? "Some are black," others "immigrants, refugees." They get

affirmative action, sympathy and welfare—"checks for the listless and idle." The government wants you to feel sorry for them.

And who runs the government? "The biracial son of a low-income single mother," and he's cheering on the line cutters. "The President and his wife are line cutters themselves." The liberal media mocks you as racist or homophobic. Everywhere you look, "you feel betrayed."

When she shared this concept with the people in her study, one said, "You've read my mind." Another remarked, "I live your analogy." They feel like strangers in their own land.

The emotions inflamed by this perspective form the "deep story"—beliefs that are more powerful than facts, no matter how clear the facts are or how often they're stated. Among these mostly middle-class white people, resentments have hardened and suspicion has taken root. One commented, "The government has gone rogue, corrupt, malicious, and ugly. It can't help anybody."[3] Hochschild's study was being concluded during

---

3. Arlie Russell Hochschild, *Strangers in Their Own Land* (New York: The New Press, 2016), p. 137, 145.

the 2016 election. It was obvious to her that candidate Donald Trump was identifying with people throughout the country who held the same views as the individuals she had studied. Millions of people resonated with his rhetoric that they were being treated unfairly, and it was time to change the entire system.

When we watch and listen to conservative news programs, we hear these refrains stated with powerful emotions and certainty. Many white people feel like victims of the progressive, godless wave of policies coming out of Washington and reinforced by the liberal media. But that's only one side of the divide. A lot of black people also feel like victims. Of course, they have historic reasons for their conclusion that the way they've been treated isn't fair. Slavery, Jim Crow laws, housing discrimination, endemic poverty, and "microaggressions" have combined to create the self-perception of being victims. One commentator calls "the victim mentality" one of the five biggest issues facing blacks in America:

Nothing holds someone back more than seeing himself as a victim. Why? Because a victim is not responsible for his situation. Everything is someone else's fault. And the victim sees little chance of improving his life. How can he get ahead if someone is holding him back? All this makes the victim unhappy, frustrated and angry.[4]

The rise of depression and anxiety in the younger generations of America is alarming. When people self-identify as victims, this perspective permeates every part of their lives and limits their hopes for the future. Unfortunately, politicians often use victimology to fuel more anger and frustration in their followers. The other side reacts in disgust, which fuels more resentment on both sides, and mutual respect continues to spiral downward.

The conclusion that life isn't fair has become pervasive in our society. We find it among whites, blacks, Hispanics, Asians, and Native Americans, rich and poor, young and old, Northerners and Southerners, coastal elites and Midwesterners. Far too often, whites believe the others are "taking our country away from us," and people of color feel the depth of white resentment and reciprocate with their own suspicion and anger. Many people of color believe whites don't want them to prosper and rise in society because white people see advancement as a "zero sum game":

---

4. "The Top 5 Issues Facing Black Americans," Taleeb Starkes, *https://assets.ctfassets.net/qnesrjodfi80/4WUqhyzxkQK2eu2asoYwgW/daebd0b44042027fb15cac0053bd127e/starkes-the_top_5_issues_facing_black_amercians-transcript.pdf*

If people of color rise, white power necessarily declines. On the other hand, whites often believe people of color have plenty of opportunities. (In fact, as Hochschild discovered, they believe people of color have an unfair level of opportunities.) In a conversation, a man remarked to me, "Slavery ended over 150 years ago. If they're still struggling, it's their fault. If they worked harder, got a good education, and made better decisions, they'd be fine. They have the same opportunities we have."

I tried to remind him that Reconstruction after the Civil War was a failure, and the Southern states were then run by the officers and soldiers who had fought for the Confederacy. The states passed a network of laws that left blacks with a degraded status little better than slavery. These "Jim Crow laws" institutionalized white supremacy with segregation in schools, business, labor, transportation, and restaurants, and severely restricted the right to vote.[5] These laws remained in effect until 1968, and the effects of almost a century of state-sponsored discrimination are still with us today. The expression on his face showed me that he wasn't interested in a history lesson. He let me know he doesn't think there's any discrimination at all against

5. For more information, see "Jim Crow Laws," February 21, 2020, History.com, *https://www.history.com/topics/early-20th-century-us/jim-crow-laws*

people of color, and particularly blacks: "If a young black man gets shot by the police, he shouldn't have talked back, he shouldn't have been wearing a hoodie, and he shouldn't have been there in the first place. He could have avoided the problem if he'd been smart." White people like him believe blacks are their own worst enemies. In other words, if they have any problems, it's entirely their fault.

The perception in the black community is starkly different. Most of the black parents I know are very careful to prepare their kids for encounters with police. They tell them, "If you're ever pulled over by the police or stopped while you're walking, do whatever they tell you to do, and do it instantly! Don't argue. Don't make excuses. Just do what they say. I don't want you to get killed." A lot of young black males are genuinely afraid that being in the wrong place at the wrong time or saying the wrong thing to the wrong person will result in the end of their lives. Black parents and their children, too, feel like strangers in their own land.

Many whites are afraid that they're losing the culture war, and liberals are taking over, ruining all they hold dear and reducing them to second-class citizens. They believe all their hard work and paying taxes are going to minorities and funding the demise of America. They're scared that blacks will move in, take over their communities, and replace wholesome neighborhoods with crime, drugs, and gangs. For this reason, when blacks begin to move into neighborhoods (primarily middle and lower-class ones), white flight begins because whites are afraid of physical harm and that their home values will decline. They're afraid Hispanics will turn the neighborhood into "little Mexico," waving Mexican flags, opening Mexican restaurants, and speaking Spanish as their only language. The Mexican culture, they're sure, will take over, creating an alternate Mexican-America within America. The prediction that whites will be in the minority in America by 2045 doesn't exactly give them comfort!

White people often feel superior to those of other races and ethnicities, which creates entitlement that the government and "those people" should treat them with much more respect. When they don't, and when it appears forces outside their control are conspiring against them, they see themselves as victims—superior victims, which seems like a very odd term but perfectly describes their perceptions.

People of color are afraid they'll never have the opportunity to thrive in our country. Whether they're black, Hispanic, Asian, or Native American, they believe they're perpetually "outside looking in" on the American dream. In addition, blacks are often hostile toward Hispanics because they believe immigrants are taking their opportunities for jobs. And today, Hispanics outnumber blacks. In many communities, there were virtually no Hispanics a few decades ago, but today they've become the second most populous ethnic group—and soon they'll surpass whites in many communities. In Texas, Hispanics are projected to surpass whites in population by 2022.[6]

People of color read reports, listen to politicians, and see the news, and they've concluded that white people genuinely don't want them here—even if they were born here. They've been second-class citizens (or perhaps undocumented), and they're afraid they'll always be unappreciated and unwanted. Images of whites carrying torches, marching and chanting hate-filled slogans make them wonder how many more aren't marching but feel the same way. The language and actions of some whites make people of color feel "less than," despised, and expendable. They live every day with a deeply rooted inferiority complex. Single-parent

---

6. "When will Latinos outnumber whites in Texas? Experts have a new prediction," Jim Cowan, *Dallas News*, June 21, 2018, *https://www.dallasnews. com/business/2018/06/21/when-will-latinos-outnumber-whites-in-texas-experts-have-a-new-prediction/*

homes produce more single-parent homes, drug abuse leads to more drug abuse, and poverty results in more poverty. The cycle seems endless—and hopeless.

Among people of color, despair is an epidemic. Poverty, lack of education, fractured families, addiction, and high crime rates make many believe that drugs, gangs, and crime are the only ways to survive. A few years ago, I met the son of a friend. The young man was only 15, but he struggled with a drug addiction. He told me that he had been dealing drugs since he was 13, and he was hooked on heroin. He had dropped out of school and was locked into a destructive, empty lifestyle—but he didn't see any way out. I tried to encourage him to make better choices and see a brighter future, and I was challenged by his response. He explained that his father was a Mexican who was in prison, and his white mother was so depressed that she was unable to hold a job to provide for them. He confidently told me, "The only way for me to survive is to deal drugs. There's no other option!" As I listened, I began to feel his pain. I realized that there were literally thousands of young people just like him who don't see any other path out of their poverty and pain. I also realized that it's very easy for me to sit back on my suburban couch and watch these stories play out on the news without ever knowing the backstory.

Fortunately, the young man's story has a happy ending. He eventually got into a recovery program and started living with an aunt who helped him get his GED and a job. However, stories like his often don't have happy endings. Hopelessness fuels an endless cycle of self-destructive choices.

The Beauty and the Challenge

"One nation, under God, indivisible, with liberty and justice for all." The Pledge of Allegiance is a powerful statement of our national identity, but in his book, *American Nations*, Colin Woodward says it's more complicated than that. He asserts, "America's most essential and abiding divisions are not between red states and blue states, conservatives and liberals, capital and labor, blacks and whites, the faithful and the secular. Rather, our divisions stem from this fact: the United States is a federation comprised in whole or in part of eleven regional nations, some of which truly do not see eye to eye with one another. ... Any effort to 'restore' fundamental American values runs into an even greater obstacle: Each of our founding cultures had its own set of cherished principles, and they often contradicted one another."[7]

Throughout our history, our government has tried to resolve differences, with some success at times and in colossal failures at others. Our diversity is a big part of what makes the United States such a wonderful country. The people who came to our shores throughout our history have been bright, motivated, and optimistic—they had to be very courageous to leave their homes and everything familiar to them to come here—and they've created an incredibly dynamic country. But their differences also have brought many challenges, and we haven't always resolved them with fairness and wisdom. We systematically expelled Native Americans from their lands, enslaved over four million blacks and when they were freed passed laws to control and use them, made immigrants from southern Europe into little more than serfs, and severely limited immigration from 1924 to 1965. Still, the United States has been a beacon of hope for people throughout the world. We've been "the

---

7. Colin Woodward, *American Nations* (New York: Penguin, 2011), Introduction.

arsenal of democracy," and the dream of millions who want a better life.

We've faced deep divisions in the past, most obviously in the 1850s and 1860s when North and South couldn't find common ground on the issue of slavery. Then, like now, animosity and distrust drowned common sense. Many people don't know that America was isolationist in the 1930s. Most of the people in this country were struggling to survive the ravages of the Great Depression and the Dust Bowl. As Europe drifted toward war and Nazi Germany gobbled up nations, many of our people preferred to believe we could stay out of the coming conflict. When the Japanese bombed Pearl Harbor, however, we mobilized our industries and our men to win the war. Calamity forged unity and propelled action.

Can we find a way to bridge the deep divide in our country today without having to face catastrophic events?

The Range of Responses

In countless conversations with people across the country in the last three decades, I've seen a range of responses to issues surrounding race. A few are radical, openly and proudly insisting on white supremacy or just as overtly demanding black power. Many are moderate, with a "live and let live" approach, but they have unspoken, strong opinions about racial preference. And some are conflicted, sensing that any kind of racism is wrong, but not clear enough or courageous enough to take a stand because they're sure they'll get substantial blowback from the radicals and even the moderates.

In the past few years, we've often heard the slogan, "Make America Great Again," but this short statement means very different things to different people. As we've seen, many white people long for the way things used to be "before the liberals passed laws infringing on our rights." They point to times when people of color knew their place and didn't rock the boat with expectations or demands. To be sure, life was simpler a few decades ago. It's easy to remember them as the best of times, but they weren't.

(By the way, I'm not taking a political stand on one side or the other. Some people who have heard me assume I'm a liberal Democrat because I'm an advocate for the disadvantaged, and some peg me as a conservative Republican because I support a number of policies that are consistent with the party. I think it's a mistake to pin the Christian label on a party. The kingdom of God is far broader, richer, and deeper than that, and besides, the people who disagree with us were, like us, made in the image of God and therefore have infinite value in His eyes ... and if we're walking with Him, in ours. I only rarely use the names of public figures, and then, to illustrate particular points, not to praise or condemn.)

But what does it mean to people of color to "Make America Great Again"? When was it great for black people? When were they, as a people, secure and prosperous? We certainly know it wasn't great when we brought countless blacks from Africa as slaves. And since slavery was abolished, has there ever been a time one could say it was great for blacks in America? We only need to think of the signs many carried during the Civil Rights movement that read, "I AM A MAN." Only decades ago, black people were so marginalized that they had to publicly claim their status as human beings! That certainly wasn't a time that generates nostalgia, unless you remember the courage of leaders like Martin Luther King, Jr., John Lewis, and Andrew Young.

When was America great for Hispanics? When the United States won the Mexican War in 1848, it acquired a large part of the Southwest, including California only a year before gold was found there. Mexican landowners had lived in these areas for generations, but many were soon marginalized: strangers in their own land. The poverty suffered in Latin American countries has, in the last decades, made a laborer's wage in the United States seem like a fortune, and millions have come to America trying to earn enough money for their families here and back home.

When was American great for Asians? Perhaps the most blatantly racist policy adopted by America after the Civil War was the Chinese Exclusion Act, which prevented any immigration from China for decades. And in the months after Pearl Harbor, President Roosevelt responded to the perceived threat of invasion and subterfuge on the West Coast by carting off people of Japanese descent to detention camps throughout the West. Some of the young men in the camps proved their loyalty to America by joining the 442nd Infantry Regiment fighting in Italy, which became the most decorated unit of its size in the war.[8] In cities throughout the country, Chinese, Japanese, Vietnamese, Koreans, and others from Asia have found safety in creating their own communities.

When was America great for Native Americans? Smallpox brought by conquistadors devastated native populations.

---

8. Kathryn Shenkle, "Patriots under Fire: Japanese Americans in World War II," United States Department of Defense, Department of the Army, Center of Military History, May 2006, *https://web.archive.org/web/20130623035411/http:/www.history.army.mil/html/topics/apam/patriots.html*

Those who survived were systematically eliminated from land that whites wanted. The Trail of Tears cost the lives of thousands who were driven from the South to Indian lands in the Oklahoma Territory, and during the gold rush in California, native people were murdered so they couldn't interfere with land claims. Tribes have established casinos to generate income, but today, Native Americans have an exceptionally high incidence of poverty, alcoholism, and drug abuse.[9]

When these people hear the plea to "Make America Great Again," they have a very different reaction than white people—for very good reasons. The people saying it seem to be saying, "Make America White Again." At least, that's how many people of color perceive it.

Who Are We?

Please don't misunderstand. I'm not saying that the complaints of white people are groundless. The shifts in culture, demographics, and policies are very real. There are real challenges with urban crime and violence, there are real challenges with border security and illegal immigration, and there are real challenges with a government

9. "Ethnicity and Health in America Series: Substance Abuse/Addiction in Native American Youth," American Psychological Association, *https://www.apa. org/pi/oema/resources/ethnicity-health/native-american/substance-use*

that wastes millions of dollars on programs that accomplish very little. It's hard to imagine how we can live in the most prosperous nation in the world but we can't seem to solve the healthcare crisis or slow the accumulation of national debt!

But if we who are white see ourselves as victims, we're forgetting who we are. When we have a sense of entitlement, we necessarily bear deep resentments. And when we're continually angry at "those people," our feet are firmly planted in the earthly culture that promises power, wealth, status, beauty, and comfort. Years ago, novelist David Foster Wallace was asked to give the commencement speech at Kenyon College. Among his advice to the graduates was the encouragement to value the right things, which always involves rejecting values that are meaningless and self-destructive. Wallace equated setting priorities with the concept of worship—our allegiance to something or someone who is most important to us. He told the audience:

> In the day-to-day trenches of adult life, there is actually no such thing as ... not worshipping. Everybody worships. The only choice we get is what to worship. And the compelling reason for maybe choosing some sort of god or spiritual-type thing to worship ... is that pretty

much anything else you worship will eat you alive. If you worship money and things, if they are where you tap real meaning in life, then you will never have enough, never feel you have enough. It's the truth. Worship your body and beauty and sexual allure and you will always feel ugly. And when time and age start showing, you will die a million deaths before they finally grieve you. ... Worship power, you will end up feeling weak and afraid, and you will need ever more power over others to numb you to your own fear. Worship your intellect, being seen as smart, you will end up feeling stupid, a fraud, always on the verge of being found out.

Wallace said that these values are "insidious" forms of worship because they're not evil or sinful, but "they're unconscious. They are default settings. They're the kind of worship you just gradually slip into, day after day, getting more and more selective about what you see and how you measure value without ever being fully aware that that's what you're doing."[10]

Does it seem odd that Wallace calls an obsession with beauty, brains, and brawn "worship"? He simply means

10. "This Is Water," David Foster Wallace, Kenyon College Commencement Address, 2005, *https://fs.blog/2012/04/david-foster-wallace-this-is-water/*

that when people value these things supremely, and devote much of their money and time to them, it's saying they have more worth than anything else.

Wallace was observing the human condition. It's completely normal for people, even Christians, to drift into the values of the earthy kingdom so much that those values dominate their hearts and minds. Unless we rigorously evaluate the ways the world squeezes us into its mold, we have little chance to embrace something higher and better than the values of our earthly culture. However, for those of us who claim Christ as Savior and Lord, there's another way, a different response: The kingdom culture provides security, peace, and wisdom, as well as the strength to speak the truth in love, have compassion for those who are unlike us, and hold people accountable in ways that build them up instead of tearing them down.

I'm afraid that many of us who are believers have segmented our hearts into the spiritual and the secular. The spiritual, we may have been taught, is about going to heaven when we die. We go to church, sing the songs, read the Bible, and pray, but we don't connect biblical truth with our expectations, our politics, and our view of people who don't look like us. Like Wallace described in his address, this perspective is actually more in alignment with the world's values than God's. I may have made you angry with some of these statements, but let me ask a question or two: Are our hearts broken by the things that break God's heart? Are we angry at the things that make Him angry?

Years ago, a pastor studied the emotions of Jesus as described in the four Gospel accounts. He found that one emotion was mentioned more than all the others combined: compassion.[11] When Jesus saw people who were hurting, grieving, lost, or overlooked, His heart went out to them. The word in the original language means for your "insides to shake." This isn't merely giving lip service about people in need; it's heartfelt, tender—yet powerful—love for those who are struggling. Jesus went out of His way to give special attention to people who were outcasts in society. He touched lepers to heal them, He picked up little children who were considered nuisances in that culture, He stopped to heal the blind and the lame, He reached out to forgive prostitutes, and He even invited himself to lunch at the home of a hated tax collector. He reached across a rigid racial barrier to love the Samaritans, and He was bitterly condemned for it. At one point when the self-righteous,

11. "The Emotional Life of our Lord," B.B. Warfield, *https://www.monergism. com/thethreshold/articles/onsite/emotionallife.html*

unloving Pharisees were angry with Him, they called Him the nastiest name they knew; they called him a Samaritan. No one was outside the sphere of His compassion. No one.

What made Jesus angry? We see flashes of anger when He found merchants turning the temple into a money-making venture. But even more, we can hear His outrage when the Pharisees, the religious leaders who should have known better, used their places of prestige to have power over the unfortunate. The Gospel writer Matthew gives us a long account of Jesus chastising them for their hardheartedness. They were, to use the term correctly, very *religious* in their behavior, but they completely missed the heart of God. For instance, Jesus criticized them: "Woe to you, scribes and Pharisees, hypocrites! For you tithe mint and dill and cumin, and have neglected the weightier matters of the law: justice and mercy and faithfulness. These you ought to have done, without neglecting the others. You blind guides, straining out a gnat and swallowing a camel!" And He condemned them for looking righteous on the outside while they had no love on the inside: "Woe to you, scribes and Pharisees, hypocrites! For you are like whitewashed tombs, which outwardly appear beautiful, but within are full of dead people's bones and all uncleanness. So you also outwardly appear righteous to others, but within you are full of hypocrisy and lawlessness" (Matthew 23:23-24, 27-28).

The question you might want to ask yourself right now is this: "Could I be a modern-day Pharisee and not even know it?"

It's a very good question, one that all of us need to have the courage to ask ourselves. Let me tease it out a little more:

- How many people of color are your true friends— not just people whose name you know and you speak to, but those you hang out with and call or text when something important happens? Or if you're a person of color, how many white people are your true friends?

- What are your instant conclusions and emotions when you watch the news and see people like you suffer at the hands of people who aren't like you?

- When you hear someone make a joke about people of another race, how do you respond?

- To what extent do you view people on the other side of the political divide as fools or evil? What words do you use to describe them? What are your emotions when you think of them, see them, or hear them?

- How do you feel about people of a different race moving into your neighborhood?
- Do you see groups like Black Lives Matter or Blue Lives Matter as all right or all wrong, or can you understand each point of view?
- Do you feel comfortable engaging in conversation with people who are different from you and welcome views that conflict with yours?
- Do you believe "Make America Great Again" and "America First" align with biblical values?

Don't make quick assumptions about these questions. Most of us have at least a twinge of cultural preference.

Today, social media is perhaps the most powerful tool in broadcasting hate. Carefully reasoned, kindhearted responses don't get much traction online, but vicious ones, fear mongering, and conspiracy theories often spread at light speed. Why are these so popular? I believe there are several reasons: online anger gives the person posting it (or sharing it) an adrenaline rush, it accentuates a power position over others, it makes the person a part of an "in-group," and it causes the person to feel completely justified in the anger. But every angry or prejudiced post is a kind of death—for the person posting and for those who read it.

The Antidote

If you're a white person, I'm sure this chapter has been hard to read because it challenges your basic assumptions of what's good and right and fair. And if you're a person of color, it challenges you to avoid "reverse discrimination" against the people you view as prejudiced against you.

Love is being willing to make adjustments for another person. In marriage, we adjust to the likes and dislikes of our spouse. In parenting, we make a million adjustments in our time, our money, and our goals to raise our kids in a way that results in competent, healthy adults. In our friendships, we make adjustments in our schedules to spend time, listen, and do things together. And in our relationships with people of other races, we make adjustments to lay our presumptions aside and value those people *as much as God values us*. In the supreme act of love, Jesus adjusted himself for us by leaving glory to become a human being, take on mortality, be ridiculed, suffer, and die so that we could have the honor, peace, and life He gives. He says, "Follow Me." That means we say what He said, feel what He felt, and do what He did. He didn't wait for outcasts to come to

Him. He pursued them. He loved them to the uttermost limit. When we love like Jesus loves, He'll pour out even more love into us.

The apostle Paul wrote a thank-you note to the believers in Philippi who had supported him on his journey to take the gospel to the world. In his letter, he got to the heart of what it means to be a follower of Christ:

Is there any encouragement from belonging to Christ? Any comfort from his love? Any fellowship together in the Spirit? Are your hearts tender and compassionate? Then make me truly happy by agreeing wholeheartedly with each other, loving one another, and working together with one mind and purpose.

Don't be selfish; don't try to impress others. Be humble, thinking of others as better than yourselves. Don't look out only for your own interests, but take an interest in others, too.

You must have the same attitude that Christ Jesus had. (Philippians 2:1-5 NLT)

Entitlement—a victim mentality that says, "It's not fair!" and resentment of others who are "cutting in line" in front of us—shows that our response to injustice isn't different from those who don't know Jesus. If we know Him ... if His love has melted and molded our hearts ... we'll give more honor to others, we'll be interested in their problems, and we'll devote ourselves to helping them rise higher. That's what it means to be motivated by love to make adjustments for others' sake.

Think About It:

What were your emotional reactions as you read this chapter?

Regarding racial issues, what are some examples of *radical* reactions? What are some examples of *moderate* responses? And what does it mean to be *conflicted* about our responses to people who are different from us?

How do the points in this chapter further illustrate the earthly culture and the kingdom culture?

What does it mean that valuing money and things, beauty, power, and intelligence are "default" positions of the human heart? Why are these values so hard to change?

How did Christ make adjustments for you? What adjustments does He want you to make for people who don't look like you?

chapter 3

Why Preference Seems Reasonable

I would argue that racial superiority in any form, white superiority as the central issue of our concern, is a heresy. The separation of human beings into ranks of superiority and inferiority differentiated by skin color is a direct assault upon the doctrine of Creation and an insult to the imago Dei—the image of God in which every human being in made. —Albert Mohler

I HAVE A FRIEND, I'll call him David, who grew up not far from our church in North Georgia. In the last few years, he's had what he calls "a revelation." I'll let him tell his story:

You could say I'm a "Son of the South." My grandmother showed me where her grandparents buried the family silver when General Sherman's cavalry rode toward Atlanta. She was still bitter about losing the war. She never called it "The Civil War" ... she said, "There was nothing civil about that war." I have a framed picture of my great-great-great-grandfather in his gray Confederate uniform.

From the time I was a little boy, I was taught by every adult in my life that the Civil War wasn't about slavery. They said secession was completely justified as "states' rights"—each state had voluntarily entered the Union, and they had the right to voluntarily leave it. If it hadn't been for Mr. Lincoln, they believed, everything would have been just fine. My grandfather was a member of the Klan. My mother showed me the exact place in the field at the family farm where he killed a black man for talking back to him. It was in the 1920s in rural Georgia, and of course, charges were never brought.

My father owned a lumber company. He was known for being unusually nice to his black employees, but he never saw them as equals. Still, they liked working for him a lot more than for other employers. When I was young, our family had maids. Nell came to work for us when she was 15 and I was in a stroller. I think we grew up together. Years later, she got married and moved to Tampa. My mother hired Rhynelle, a tiny woman whose husband was in the state prison in Reidsville for a double murder. During the Civil Rights movement, when blacks were encouraged to have more pride in their identity, things got pretty tense around our house. One afternoon, my mother was ready to take Rhynelle home at the end of the day, and Rhynelle opened the door of the front seat and got in. I thought my mother would blow a gasket, but she didn't make her get in the back.

One day when I traveled to the farm to look around, I decided to visit a man who had been a share cropper on the land for many years. He was probably close to 80 at that point, and he lived alone in a small, clapboard house on the property. I knocked on the door, introduced myself, and he invited me in. For the next half hour, I got a glimpse of a man who had worked hard all his life for a pittance, who had, through years of cultural training, always deferred to white people, but who proudly hung three pictures on his wall: John Kennedy, Martin Luther King, Jr., and Jesus. For me, our meeting was both moving and sad.

For many years, I read Civil War history. My parents gave me an original edition of Douglas Southhall Freeman's Pulitzer Prize winning biography of Robert E. Lee. I have a shelf full of histories and biographies, all extolling the virtues of valiant Southern leaders as they fought against the unrighteous Yankees. I often talked to friends about the noble Christians like Lee and Stonewall Jackson ... and the godless Northern generals.

I hate to say it, but my views of the war, slavery, and the place of black people remained unchanged for decades. Then, when I was in my 60s, my wife heard a radio interview with Bruce Levine, the author of a book titled *The Fall of the House of Dixie.* It was a revelation. I read the book three times. For the first time in my life, I saw the injustice of the Southern cause, the cruelty of slavery, and the ends the South was willing to go to, to keep black people enslaved. Decades of assumptions melted away. I read *Just Mercy* by Bryan Stevenson, about racial injustice in the prison system, and I read *Blood at the Root,* an account of a lynching and the expulsion of every black person from Forsyth County, Georgia— an exile that lasted almost 70 years until a few blacks began to move back to the county. I read *The Warmth of Other Suns,* the story of black migration after World War I until the 1970s from the oppressive culture of the South to the promise of better conditions and opportunities in the North and West. It was like the scales had been peeled off my eyes, and I couldn't get enough of the new perspective.

One of my friends is interested and supportive of the change, but most of the people who have heard me explain my new views are at least suspicious ... and many are angry. I understand. I would have been suspicious, too, a few years ago. I don't think it's too much to say that it feels like I've been born again—again. I've never considered myself to be a racist. I think I've been nice to people of color, but that's not the same thing as seeing them as equals. I still have a long way to go, but I'm working on it.

The Spectrum

In my own experience and from talking to many people about racial reconciliation, we can identify a range of five distinct responses: inclusion, paternalism, preference, intolerance, and racism.

Inclusion: Seeing all people as equally valuable; caring equally about every person, regardless of race, color, religion, or national origin; and respecting differences without demanding people conform to our tastes. This is how Jesus treated people.

Paternalism: Being nice, but in a condescending way. Viewing ourselves as superior. This is how David's father treated black people who worked for him. In *I'm Still Here: Black Dignity in a World Made for Whiteness*, Austin Channing Brown observes, "When you believe niceness disproves the presence of racism, it's easy to start believing bigotry is rare, and that the label *racist* should be applied only to mean-spirited, intentional acts of discrimination."[12]

Preference: Making the evaluation that our race and culture is better. Making no attempt to harm people who aren't like us, but having no desire to explore relationships with "them."

Intolerance: Making assumptions that "those people" threaten us—as individuals and as a race. Filtering the news through a very strong bias against people who aren't like us.

---

12. Austin Channing Brown, *I'm Still Here: Black Dignity in a World Made for Whiteness* (New York: Convergent Books, 2018), p. 101.

Racism: Seeing our race as superior and others as inferior. Joining with others to reinforce bigotry and hatred. Marching and taking other public stands.

I see the people in our nation—and the people in our churches—on a bell curve, with relatively few people on either end of loving inclusion or hateful racism, more who are patronizing or intolerant, and a lot in the middle showing preference but without powerful feelings of love or revulsion.

For many, preference makes perfect sense. We don't see any need to change because we're just letting people live their lives and hoping they'll let us live ours. After all, we're not marching with swastikas, we're not in the Klan and burning crosses on the lawns of courthouses, and we're not spewing hatred and slogans of racial supremacy—and we don't openly condone those who do. We don't want to rock the boat with any major changes in society. There are enough problems already! And if we reevaluate our position on race, our friends might accuse us of being traitors to our kind. Heaven forbid! Many of us secretly see our race as "better than," "more responsible than," and "more noble than," but we don't say it out loud. We just prefer to be with people who look like us, cook like us, talk like us, and see the world the way we do. It's much more comfortable that way.

When David was with some friends, one of them asked him, "What do you think about all the debate about Confederate statues?"

David paused for a second to consider how his new position would sound, but he decided to wade in anyway. He told them, "Actually, I've changed my views in the past couple of years. As all of you know, I've been an advocate of the South all my life, but I've had to ask myself this question: 'If I stood with a black man in front of one of these statues, how could I defend the history of using military force to keep his people enslaved?' I just can't do it. I know there are black historians who advocate keeping the Confederate statues but having an additional display to explain 'the other side.' That might work, but at this point, I'm afraid the statues honor a culture that had a dishonorable cause." It didn't take long for the guys to react. "One of them barked at me, 'You're betraying your heritage!' And another actually came out of his seat, leaned toward me and yelled, 'You're denying our history!' I told him, 'No, not at all. I'm affirming the truth about our history.'" David's move on the spectrum came at a price.

Rationalizations

Tradition has a powerful pull on us. It's easy to avoid asking hard questions because we don't even think to ask them. When I lived in Richmond, I lived on Monument Avenue, a street lined with statues of Confederate heroes. My house was directly in front of the statue of Robert E. Lee on his horse, Traveler. But the whole time I lived there, I never thought about the implications of the street and the statues. They were just there. Only later did I realize what they symbolize for people whose ancestors had been owned by Southern leaders. It's strange now to see this statue and several others in Richmond coming down as our nation starts to face the reality of what they represent. For the first time, the question is finally being asked: "Why are we honoring people who fought against the United States to preserve slavery?"

Like David described in his story, sometimes we need a jolt to move us on the spectrum. Another friend called me a few years ago right after tragic events happened back-to-back involving racial issues. In July of 2016, two black men were shot and killed by police within a day of each other in Minnesota and Louisiana. Their names were Philando Castile and Alton Sterling. In response, demonstrations were held in both states, including in my friend's city of Dallas to protest what was considered excessive force by the officers involved. During the protest in Dallas, Micah Johnson made his way to the top of a nearby building and opened fire on the police who were walking with the marchers. Eleven officers were shot, and five were killed. At my friend's church the next Sunday, the pastor talked about the horror of the murder of the police, but he didn't say anything about what prompted the march—the deaths of the two black men and the pattern of blacks dying at the hands of white officers. I remember these events very clearly. Our family was on vacation in Florida, and we had to hurry back, so I could address this senseless racial violence. It was a very tense time in our country. When I spoke to our church, I tried to help both sides understand and empathize with the other's pain. My friend told me that he was very disappointed in his church because the pastor and the people didn't grasp the long history of racial profiling by the police. He told me that after hearing me talk about it, he began to see that his church was unwilling to feel the pain of black America. He finally realized he could no longer stay silent. From that point, he decided to speak up, even at the expense of losing some of his friends.

Before the Civil War, denominations argued about slavery, and that's when Baptists, Presbyterians, and other groups split into Northern and Southern factions. Pastors in the South preached that slavery was God's will, and they found passages to support their position. Then and later, "scientists" used phrenology (the study of the shape of the head) and eugenics (a view, later used by Nazi Germany, to prove that the white race is superior to others) and other theories to justify racism. In his book, *Shattering the Myth of Race: Genetic Realities and Biblical Truths*, biology professor Dave Unander explains:

> Race is mostly a social theory that was devised and refined over the centuries to serve the economic and religious goals of a majority culture, first in European territory, then later in America. Whiteness, it turns out, is a very recent idea in the grand scheme of history, but it's a powerful one that was used to create categories and systems that would place value, economically and otherwise, on skin color and the groups of people who were either blessed or burdened by it. If race could be used to indicate a group's level of intelligence, its work ethic, and its tendency to do wrong, then the majority culture could justify all types of bigotries and discriminations.[13]

13. Dave Unander, *Shattering the Myth of Race: Genetic Realities and Biblical Truths* (Judson Press, 2000).

This isn't an ancient phenomenon. Today, white nationalists are on the rise. Black Lives Matter was a reaction to the deaths of so many young black men at the hands of police, and the counterpoint to it is Blue Lives Matter, defending the police. Over 1,000 hate groups are active in the United States, 30 percent more than just four years earlier. In 2018, right-wing extremists were responsible for at least 50 killings; Muslim jihadist groups were linked to none.[14] Alarmingly, armed militias are growing. In a PBS report, P. J. Tobia commented:

> There are more than 500 militia groups in the U.S., more than double the number in 2008, according to the Anti-Defamation League. Most of them are right-wing and anti-government. In addition to the 3 Percent Militia, there's the Oath Keepers, formed in 2009. They're primarily current and former law enforcement and military personnel. Oath Keepers showed up in Ferguson, Missouri, during the protests in the summer of 2015. They said they were there to help keep the peace and protect reporters working for the conspiracy-fueled Web site Infowars. Meanwhile, thousands have flocked

14. "Over 1,000 Hate Groups Are Now Active in United States, Civil Rights Group Says," Liam Stack, *New York Times*, February 20, 2019, *https://www. nytimes.com/2019/02/20/us/hate-groups-rise.html*

to older groups like the Sovereign Citizens Movement, tax resisters who deny the legitimacy of the American government.[15]

These people assure us they're only protecting the America they love—a white America where they feel empowered to hate.

As I write this chapter, the nation is trying to cope with the killing of Ahmaud Arbery. He was jogging down a street in a suburb of Brunswick, Georgia. A former detective and his son suspected that he was a burglar, so they plotted a citizen's arrest. They enlisted a friend to drive behind Arbery and herd him toward their pickup blocking the street in his path. He was wearing shorts and a t-shirt. He held nothing in his hands. Still, the two men confronted him, and in an altercation, Arbery was killed with a shotgun blast. Conservative columnist David French, observes that this and similar deaths of young black men follow a clear pattern—for illustration, he used Trayvon Martin, Philando Castile, and Arbery. In each case, an "unreasonable fear" propelled white people to see a threat when there was none. They took dramatic action, using lethal violence instead of

15. "Why armed militia groups are surging across the nation," P. J. Tobias and Judy Woodruff, *PBS Newshour*, April 19, 2017, *https://www.pbs.org/newshour/show/armed-militia-groups-surging-across-nation*

calling the police to investigate. In Castile's case, a policeman shot and killed him in his car even though Castile was
calmly saying that he had a gun and a concealed handgun
license. It didn't matter. The officer's initial suspicion quickly mushroomed into heightened fear and deadly action.

The response of many white conservatives, is to defend
the assailants and blame the victims. French writes,

> Rather than rightly being seen as a badge of shame, the
> shooters' paranoia unites their defenders in righteous
> indignation. How can this be? In part because a part
> of the U.S. population shares the same perceptions of
> threat as the shooters themselves. ... Put another way,
> there are Americans who would never pick up a weap-
> on and try to track down a black man running on the
> street—or follow a young black man on a rainy night—
> but they understand and sympathize with those who
> do.[16]

I would guess that those who sympathize with the mo-
tives for this kind of senseless violence appear on the surface to show *preference* to their white race but are secretly
intolerant. They don't spew racial venom, but they don't

---

16. "The double injustice of unreasonable fear," David French, *TIME*, June 1-8,
2020, p. 29.

distance themselves from the people who do. In fact, they defend them. I'm afraid more people are intolerant than I'd like to believe.

Our country has seen periodic spasms of race rioting. Most of these started with legitimate protests, usually of a black man killed by police, but in too many cases, the understandable grief and anger of the many in the streets provided an opportunity to incite chaos by a few. In "The Case Against Riots," columnist Ross Douthat looked back at the nonviolent protests during the Civil Rights movement:

> More broadly, in news coverage and public opinion from those years, nonviolent protests (especially in the face of segregationist violence) increased support for civil rights while violent protests tipped public opinion away from the protesters, and toward a stronger desire for what Nixon called law and order.

More recently, agitators have used peaceful protests to incite rage and destruction, including throwing Molotov cocktails, burning cars and businesses, and looting stores. Any sympathy that would have been won by the peaceful protests is effectively wiped out by scenes of violence. Douthat cites a study by writer Jonathan Chait conducted in 2015 when riots broke out in Ferguson, Missouri, after the killing of Michael Brown and in Baltimore, Maryland, after Freddie Gray died in the back of a police van. Chait accused the pro-riot radicals of being delusional in their belief that riots produce positive change:

> The physical damage inflicted upon poor urban neighborhoods by rioting, does not have the compensating virtue of easing the way for more progressive policies; instead, it compounds the damage by promoting a regressive backlash.[17]

I've seen how this violence changes the perception of white people. Many have growing empathy for the senseless deaths of blacks at the hands of white law enforcement, but their empathy immediately vanishes when they watch news clips of enraged protesters attacking police, burning everything in sight, and carrying big screen televisions out of vandalized stores. I can almost read their thoughts: *See, that's what they're really like. How can I be sympathetic toward people who are so lawless and destructive? There's no hope for them.* Their intolerance is again confirmed by the images of looting and destruction.

---

17. "The Case Against Riots," Ross Douthat, *New York Times*, May 30, 2020, *https://www.nytimes.com/2020/05/30/opinion/sunday/riots-george-floyd.html*

To Be Fair

We all—no matter our color, ethnicity, or background—generally have a preference for our own kind, and we're suspicious of those who are different from us. I've said enough about the spectrum among whites from loving, intentional inclusion to vicious racism, but we need to understand that the same range applies to people of color. Many have been attracted to our church because they feel welcome and even honored. This is a novel experience for a lot of them. But blacks, Hispanics, Asians, and Native Americans can be just as guilty of intolerance and racism as whites. Some call this "reverse racism" or "reverse discrimination." In this case, whites believe that attempts to correct inequality are forms of anti-white racism. In recent years, organizations like Black Lives Matter have led protests against police killings of young black men. Observers argue that at least some of the blacks are going beyond advocating legal redress of injustice. In their outrage, they seem to paint all whites with the brush of willful prejudice, just like many whites paint all people of color with the brush of inferiority.

Suspicion, fear, intolerance, and racism are a toxic brew on both sides. Unfortunately, the liberal media generally portrays people of color as victims, and the conservative media returns the favor by presenting people of color as unreasonable and demanding—and whites as victims.

Generational Split

I've seen very different views on race among those who are older than 50 and those who are younger than 40. People near my age grew up in a segregated society, or in one that was full of tension as integration gradually happened. We remember the race riots in the Watts neighborhood in Los Angeles, the burning of cities after Martin Luther King, Jr., was assassinated, the polarization of the OJ trial, and the nightly news reports of drugs, crime, and gang violence in poverty-ridden parts of cities. Black outrage was immediately joined by white outrage *at their outrage*, and the poles widened. White people assumed their race was superior because, by every measurement in society and the economy, it was. This assumption inevitably made the superior judgmental and the inferior resentful—which reinforced each other. With this attitude, preference (if not intolerance) has been very natural and reasonable, and the races have remained separate.

In contrast, young people have grown up in an integrated society. They're used to being around people of different races, so it's easier to have friends who don't look like them. The older generation is horrified and mystified by interracial marriages; but to the young, it's no big deal. Older people rail about the Supreme Court allowing gay marriage, and they fret that gays are so visible in commercials, movies, television, the theatre, and other segments of society. But they don't realize that when they're so fiercely critical of gay people, they're talking about their children's friends. The same pattern exists in how each group views issues of race: The prejudice of older people is driving young people away.

Entrenched Inequality

The playing field in America where races compete consists of education, housing, healthcare, and employment opportunities. The gap in household wealth between whites and people of color is a reflection of centuries of white privilege. In fact, black wealth has actually declined in the past three decades.[18] A Pew Research Center study found that "Americans generally think being white is an advantage in society, while about half or more say being black or Hispanic hurts people's ability to get ahead."[19]

---

18. "Racial Economic Inequality," *https://inequality.org/facts/racial-inequality/*

19. "Views of racial inequality," Juliana Menasce Horowitz, Anna Brown, and Kiana Cox, Pew Research Center, April 9, 2019, *https://www.pewsocialtrends.org/2019/04/09/views-of-racial-inequality/*

These conclusions aren't based only in statistics. This set of expectations has been formed and hardened over many years in endless interactions that communicated I'm up and you're down or I'm down and you're up. And they can mean the difference between life and death. A study conducted by the Century Foundation and reported by Jamila Taylor found that blacks have seen some gains in healthcare, but their situation is still precarious:

Increases in health insurance coverage under the ACA [The Affordable Care Act, also known as Obamacare] have improved access to medical care and have been linked to better outcomes for African Americans, such as earlier diagnosis and treatment of certain cancers. However, disparities still exist across health conditions when comparing African Americans and whites, including maternal mortality, infant mortality, heart disease, diabetes, cancer, and other health issues. Social factors, including economic disadvantage, inequities in education, and lack of access to health care, impact a person's ability to lead a healthy and productive life. For people in American society that experience racism and inequality in their daily lives, and throughout the lifespan, the impact of social factors on health are the most grave.[20]

For the white people in Hochschild's study of conservatives in Louisiana, having people of color "cut in line" inflamed outrage at the injustice. However, for generations many people of color haven't been able to even find the line.

God has created us with a thirst for justice. Even little children are quick to say, "That's not fair!" And we still say it—more loudly and frequently—when we're older. Today, some are calling for reparations to compensate blacks for the impact of slavery that still persists today. This demand has precedence: In 2010, the U.S. government paid $3.4 billion to settle a class-action lawsuit filed by Native Americans. The suit represented people who "subsist in the direst poverty," and in the view of the attorney for the tribes, the settlement was "significantly less than the full amount to which the Indians are owed." The payment wasn't called reparations, but it was a tangible, monetary form of justice for Native Americans. However, there are several problems with the modern black demand for reparations: All of the enslaved people are now deceased, so

---

20 "Racism, Inequality, and Health Care for African Americans," Jamila Taylor, The Century Foundation, December 19, 2019, *https://tcf.org/content/report/racism-inequality-health-care-african-americans/?session=1*

they can't be beneficiaries. And how would a fair amount be calculated, how would it be distributed, and what impact would it have on race relations? Is there a better way to level the playing field?

Hispanics don't have a history of slavery in America, but they believe their contribution to America, largely through their work in restaurants, on farms, and in construction, should open the door to a path to citizenship and government assistance to help care for their families. They are very hardworking people, and they believe justice requires action on their behalf. In response, many whites insist that the ones who are here illegally have effectively eliminated themselves from this consideration.

Recently I studied the Great Depression to see if there are any correlations between then and now. The stock market crash in October of 1929 was the first major sign that the economy was in trouble. Speculation had driven stock prices up, far beyond the actual value of the companies. The collapse of banks, farms, distribution, and earning power—all of which led to massive unemployment with virtually no safety net—came after the Roaring Twenties, a time of unbridled optimism and incredible wealth accumulated by a few, the vast majority of whom were white.

Like we've seen during the economic problems created by the COVID-19 pandemic, the pain of the Great Depression was felt disproportionately by the working class. The nation had an unemployment rate up to 25% and 50% for blacks. In Atlanta, 70% of blacks couldn't find jobs. During the 30s, the rich may have seen a decline in their portfolios, but they retained enough in reserve to ride out the Depression in style. To save their money, they pulled back on investments which would have created jobs for the poor. President Roosevelt stepped into office during the worst of the crisis. Banks were closing every day, wiping out the savings of countless people. He declared a "bank holiday" that let people catch their breath and make decisions based on something other than raw panic. He also began sending bills to Congress to create government-funded, government-run programs to put people back to work, so they could afford basic necessities. His motto was simple: "Take a method and *try* it. If it fails, admit it frankly, and *try* another. But by all means, *try something.*" He launched the Civilian Conservation Corps, the Civil Works Administration, the Works Projects Administration, the National Youth Administration, and many other job-creating programs.

Since 1924, immigration had been severely restricted, so the predominate minority in the country were blacks. In the Depression, not only did they suffer much higher unemployment, but when they found jobs, they were paid a fraction of the wages whites received. The inherent racial views of white Americans gave them no incentive to push for equity in pay for blacks. They may not have been in the Klan, and they may not have been "hard racists," but they weren't concerned enough to address the problem. They were what I call "soft racists," showing preference for their own kind. Today, the problem is a stubborn root in our culture. During the last two and a half decades, median household wealth for whites rose by 30%, and it increased for Hispanics by 50%, but black household wealth shrank by 50%.[21] On conservative cable news, wealthy, successful blacks are showcased as examples of what they can do "if they just apply themselves," but these are exceptions that prove the rule: There aren't many of them because they don't have as many opportunities to advance. For them, it takes exceptional talent, drive, and at least one open door for them to find extraordinary success.

---

21. "Why Racial Economic Disparity Keeps Growing in the U.S.," Dwyer, Gunn, *Pacific Standard*, January 16, 2019, *https://psmag.com/economics/why-racial-economic-disparity-keeps-growing-in-the-us*

People in the middle of the spectrum, those in the preference range, believe the playing field is level, and people of color have exactly the same opportunities as whites. They don't, but most whites aren't interested in hearing the other side. These whites assume that blacks believe the lie told by liberals that they're victims, and they can't make it without advantages doled out by the government. That's why they stay poor.

Actually, I believe there's truth on both sides: Some blacks do see themselves as helpless victims, and they need to take more responsibility for their lives, but the ingrained racial inequity in our culture is also very real. Neither truth should be denied.

Not Enough

I attended a pastors' conference a few years ago that was designed to promote racial understanding and harmony in response to heightened tensions from police shootings of young black men. The pastors were from black, Hispanic, and white churches across the country. The black speakers focused their outrage on whites who hadn't provided enough opportunities for blacks in their communities. They pleaded with white leaders to help them. The white speakers spent most of their time apologizing for the way blacks and

Hispanics have been treated in America. They pledged to do better. That was it: black anger and white guilt, but no action steps to move people toward reconciliation. I discovered that none of the speakers had a racially diverse church, so they weren't doing anything (visible anyway) about the problem. People walked away from the conference either validated in their anger or ashamed that their people had been so uncaring, but very little if anything actually changed.

The solutions proposed by national leaders aren't working. Some incite division by harsh words about "black ghettos" in big cities and unwanted immigrants, and the other side tries to look noble by pouring money into those cities and defending immigrants, especially those who are here illegally. The solution to racism and intolerance isn't passive preference. That's not good enough. On April 2, 1963, Dr. Martin Luther King, Jr., was arrested in Birmingham, Alabama. Eight white pastors wrote a letter titled "A Call for Unity," that was published in the newspaper, condemning Dr. King's method of nonviolent resistance. In response, he wrote his famous "Letter from Birmingham Jail." In part, it reads:

I must make two honest confessions to you, my Christian and Jewish brothers. First, I must confess that

over the past few years I have been gravely disappointed with the white moderate. I have almost reached the
regrettable conclusion that the Negro's great stumbling
block in the stride toward freedom is not the White
Citizen's Counciler or the Ku Klux Klanner, but the
WHITE MODERATE, who is more devoted to "order"
than to justice; who prefers a negative peace which is the
absence of tension to a positive peace which is the presence of justice; who constantly says: "I agree with you in
the goal you seek but I cannot agree with your methods
of direct action"; who paternalistically believes he can
set the timetable for another man's freedom; who lives
by a mythical concept of time and who constantly ad-
vises the Negro to wait for a "more convenient season."

Like Dr. King, I'm disappointed with white moderates.
We see images of white racists marching, but most of us
can easily dismiss them as the radical right. The real problem is that the vast majority of white people aren't moved
by injustice, don't stand up for those in need, and have no
stomach to make the hard changes that can provide equal
opportunities. It's our responsibility to step into the gap, to
help people rise up by teaching them to manage money,
apply for a job, or get more education. We've made some

progress over the years to institute fair hiring practices, admit more minorities to universities through affirmative action, and other advances, but in my experience, most white leaders don't even have racial inequity and social justice on their radars—it may be a crying need to a few, but for many it doesn't even register.

We can do more. We must do more.

As examples of specific steps we can take, allow me to share what we've done in two areas over the last few years at Victory:

Education

When I think about how to help minorities get an equal footing in America, one of the first things that comes to mind is education. I think most people underestimate the power of education and how it affects a person's ability to succeed.

Several years ago, I sensed God speaking to me about this issue. I believed He was calling our church to start a private school that would provide minorities with a top-tier education as well as instill Christian values. The idea was to hire top educators and create a school that gives minorities the same chance as children like I had when I was growing up. The school was a part of our mission to the community, so in the beginning, we contributed a significant amount of funds so that single mothers and low-income families could afford to enroll their children. After several years and the work of many dedicated people, Victory World Christian School became the only school in the world to have all four of the top accreditations: ACSI, International Baccalaureate, Cognia Advanced Ed, and Cognia STEM certification. The students grade out annually two and three grades ahead and have become a part of the Duke Tip program, which recognizes the top 5% of students in the nation. These honors were accomplished with 90% black and brown children who were given an equal opportunity!

Healthcare

Perhaps nothing speaks louder about the reality of inequality than the plight of healthcare for minorities. A few years ago, I had dinner with a black friend, Dr. Leroy Graham. We discussed what we could do to bring better healthcare to the black and brown community around our church. We concluded that the church must be a part of the solution, so we raised about $750,000 to start this effort. With the help of around 240 medical volunteers, we launched Bridge Atlanta Medical Center. Today, after a few years of development and merging with Good

Samaritan, we're seeing about 500 patients a week who can't afford health insurance. The real blessing is that they are seeing some of the top doctors in the state, gifted and compassionate physicians who are retired but volunteer their services part time.

I often imagine what it would look like if every church in America became a part of the solution to inequality instead of expecting the government to fix all the problems. The church can lead the way. If we do, I believe the rest of the community will follow. This is a way God's people can show love to people who are different, who have been marginalized, and who wonder if we really care. Recently, there has been a lot of talk about reparations to right the wrongs of the past. Maybe the church's kindness, inclusion, and generosity will be considered a form of reparations to make up for our blindness and sins of the past.

Think About It:

How would you describe each of the five points on the spectrum?

- Inclusion
- Paternalism
- Preference
- Intolerance
- Racism

Where are you on the scale? Explain your answer.

If you're over 50, what kind of conversations about race do you have with the younger generation? If you're under 40, what kind of conversations do you have with your parents and grandparents?

What's entirely reasonable about preference in racial views? What's wrong with it?

Do you believe there is racial inequality in America? Why or why not?

What would make you willing—and even eager—to move up the scale toward inclusion?

chapter 4

Love Conquers All

A Rattlesnake, if cornered will become so angry it will bite itself. That is exactly what the harboring of hate and resentment against others is—a biting of oneself. We think we are harming others in holding these spites and hates, but the deeper harm is to ourselves. —E. Stanley Jones

VERY EARLY IN my career, I tried to figure out what kind of church God wanted us to build, As I read the Bible, the theme of racial division and reconciliation appeared again and again. It seemed to be pretty important to God! Many familiar passages jumped off the page. One of these was a statement Jesus made to His followers a few hours before He was betrayed and arrested on trumped-up charges. He told them, "Let me give you a new command: Love one another. In the same way I loved you, you love one another. This is how everyone will recognize that you are my disciples—when they see the love you have for each other" (John 13:34-35, MSG). Why did He say it was "a new command"? Hadn't they read plenty of passages in the Bible about love? Yes, but Jesus upped the level. What was new was the quality and breadth of the love they were to share with each other. They were to love one another "in the same way I loved you"—intentionally, sacrificially, and passionately, overcoming every form of suspicion and prejudice. They would remember this moment a few weeks later. Jesus had risen from the dead and appeared to them for 40 days. As we've seen, just before He ascended, He told them to reach out beyond the Jewish people, to invite the Samaritans into their new family of God, and to go to everyone on the planet to take them the Good News of Jesus' expansive love.

I realized it was always in the heart of God for His love to reconcile people first to himself and then to each other—wherever they've come from, whatever they look like, however they've lived. In fact, in Genesis when God chose Abraham to get His plan back on track after a disastrous beginning, He promised:

> I'll make you a great nation
>   and bless you.
> I'll make you famous;
>   you'll be a blessing.

I'll bless those who bless you;
 those who curse you I'll curse.
All the families of the Earth
 will be blessed through you. (Genesis 12:2-3, MSG)

"All the families of the Earth" meant and means not just one race, not just one nation, not just one ethnic group, everybody. God doesn't love white people more than black people, or Asians more than Hispanics, or Jews more than Gentiles. All are welcome into His family.

For believers in our country, we still have a lot of work to do. We call it the United States of America, but we're anything but united. It's understandable that unbelievers jockey for power, prestige, pleasure, and possessions. We see it on a larger scale with bitter arguments between blue states and red states, Democrats and Republicans in Congress, and polarized views on virtually every important policy. We see it at the personal level, especially on social media, as individuals jump on bandwagons and join with others to condemn those who don't agree with them. That's the nature of an unredeemed human heart. But what about people in God's family? Why is there so much anger and divisive language from those to claim to have been changed by the love of God? As I've said, I'm convinced that many of us are far more influenced by the world's values than God's values. I also believe there are unseen forces at work: forces of light and forces of darkness. The forces of light invite us to love like Jesus loves; the forces of darkness sow negative assumptions which quickly turn hearts cold. Which side is reflected in our attitudes, our behavior, our words, and our posts?

Inside Out

The forces of light transform us from the inside out. In Paul's second letter to the Christians in Corinth, he explained how this transformation happens. He begins by driving a stake into the center of the issue. Without the experience of Christ's love, transformation doesn't even begin:

> For the love of Christ controls us, because we have concluded this: that one has died for all, therefore all have died; and he died for all, that those who live might no longer live for themselves but for him who for their sake died and was raised.

Paul then says that the power of Jesus' cross has given him new eyes to view every person:

> From now on, therefore, we regard no one according to the flesh [race, national origin, or natural talents]. Even

though we once regarded Christ according to the flesh, we regard him thus no longer.

When we enter God's family through grace alone, faith alone, and Christ alone, a miracle happens inside us:

Therefore, if anyone is in Christ, he is a new creation. The old has passed away; behold, the new has come.

But that's not all. After we're reconciled to God, we have the incredible honor of being His hands, feet, and voice to invite others to be reconciled to Him, and when they are, they're reconciled to us, too.

All this is from God, who through Christ reconciled us to himself and gave us the ministry of reconciliation; that is, in Christ God was reconciling the world to himself, not counting their trespasses against them, and entrusting to us the message of reconciliation. Therefore, we are ambassadors for Christ, God making his appeal through us. We implore you on behalf of Christ, be reconciled to God. For our sake he made him to be sin who knew no sin, so that in him we might become the righteousness of God (2 Corinthians 5:14-21).

An ambassador represents his country to the people of a foreign land. For him to be effective, he has to go there, become fluent in the language, and learn the customs of the people in that country. He doesn't stand on the shore of his native land and yell that the people in the other country are crazy. His job—his privilege—is to immerse himself in the other culture, so he can understand its people, speak effectively to them, and build bridges between the two nations. That's our job, too, in our relationship to people of other races, cultures, and nations.

In my book, *10: Qualities that Transform a Basic Believer into a Committed Disciple*, I described "four dimensions of love," that makeup the kind of love Jesus demonstrated for all people. When our hearts are captured by the incredible love of God, we realize He knows the very worst about us and loves us still, and though we're deeply flawed, He considers us to be His treasure—more valuable than the stars in the sky and all the jewels in the earth. When this love melts our hearts, our defenses go down, our excuses evaporate, and we resemble Jesus in our relationships. We love *the least*: the poor, the sick, prisoners, and others who have no way to repay us for our kindness and generosity. We love *the lost*: people who don't know God, whose lifestyles may be quite unattractive, and whose choices reflect the selfishness that's deeply rooted in every human heart. We love *across cultures*: people on the other side of the world, but also those on the other side of town (and maybe up the street). And we love our *enemies*: people who have betrayed us, abused us, abandoned us, or offended us in any way. Our tendency is to value only people who are like us, who are respectable, and who don't make us uncomfortable, but in all four dimensions of love, we see people the way Jesus sees them, not with our normal perception, but through the lens of His grace.

We can go to church for decades but never have a changed heart or a changed perspective about people. But when the love of Christ compels us and we're stunned that He would love us so much that He would come to sacrifice himself for us, an internal transformation gives us a new heart, new eyes, and a new purpose. New believers need to mature in their faith, so this transformation changes their relationships, and stuck believers need God to shake them out of their complacency. One of the primary evidences that a person has been born again is a transformed heart that loves the least, the lost, across cultures, and enemies. Someone may not have been taught that racial reconciliation is God's idea, but someone who is born again will be open to it and eager to please God in this area of life.

Early in my study of racial reconciliation, I sensed God ask me, "Dennis, do you really love black people as much as you love white people?" I could honestly answer, "Yes, I love black and white equally." God asked me the same question about Hispanics, and then about Asians. Each time, I realized God wanted me to look deeper into my heart and not just gloss over this question. I realized that for the first time in my life, I felt an overwhelming love for people from other cultures. If you'd known me before I met Christ, you'd have a difficult time believing this about me, but Jesus has changed me. After I answered, the Lord asked me another question. This time, it was more practical and personal: "If you lead your church toward racial reconciliation, and a lot of white people leave the church, will you stay and be a loving, contented pastor for whomever I send to your church?" I knew this wasn't a random, hypothetical question. It was a real possibility in North Georgia. I responded, "Yes, I'll stay, and yes, I'll pastor whomever you send me, Lord."

A few years later, when our part of the city became more integrated, many of the predominantly white churches moved farther north so their people wouldn't have to change their views on race relations. Their decision disheartened me because it was a loud and clear message to people of color that they weren't welcome in these church-es. The pastors and church leaders may have insisted the move had nothing to do with race, but I don't believe it. They sold their church buildings and moved to areas where their members were finding new homes and, once again, segregating themselves from other races. We stayed be-cause we believe that all people are valuable to God. It was the best decision our church has ever made!

At the time, my daughter Lauren attended a private Christian school that was all white. As she was about to enter high school, I met with the principal to ask him if the school had a vision to reach out to the minority com-munities and make the school more integrated. He told me that this concept had never been a part of the vision of the parents and school leaders, and it probably wasn't going to happen any time in the near future. After I learned this fact, I talked with Lauren, and we decided it was time for her to go to a public school where she would be around people of other races and do life with them every day.

Soon after classes began, Lauren saw why a school needs to be integrated. In her senior year, she decided to run for school president to have more influence. She told me she probably didn't have a chance because she wasn't as popular as some of the students who were running, but she felt the Lord urging her to try. She explained that each candidate had to give a seven-minute speech before the election, so I suggested that she talk about the importance of reconciling the races. We wrote her speech together, and she gave it the next day. I'll never forget the call when she told me what happened after she gave the speech. She said that God seemed to touch her in a special way, and that every student was engaged because it spoke to the challenges the public school was having. She got a standing ovation, and in the vote, she won in a landslide! This message resonates with young people today, but many parents don't take the time to get involved. I often think about what it would look like if more parents taught their children the importance of this issue and encouraged them to be a part of the solution instead of the problem.

Government isn't the solution for racial tensions and inequity. Changed hearts are the answer, and the only one who can make that happen is Jesus. The experience of His amazing love changes us so that we think, feel, and act in ways that build connections with people. When we expect government to solve this problem, we'll inevitably stand on one side or the other, making demands and blaming those who don't agree with us. I'm not suggesting government has no role to play. Federal, state, and local officials can advocate policies that create opportunities for all people to rise out of poverty, enjoy safety and security, and have access to education and healthcare. I'm certainly for these interventions, but even the very best policies don't make people kind, gracious, and loving.

Rise Above

One of the beautiful things about social media is that we can instantly connect with so many people about virtually anything. Perhaps the ugliest thing about it is that the connections too often take the form of venomous words spewing hate about anything and everything. If we want to walk in the love of God and reach out to people, we have to learn to rise above offenses, to be strong enough to keep moving forward and humble enough to move with compassion instead of resentment.

In 2016 while I was teaching a message on racial reconciliation, I asked a young black man to come on stage so I could wash his feet. I spent time explaining that God had worked in my heart to give me a love for every race, and I told him that washing his feet was a symbol of my commitment to clean the part that gets dirty just from ordinary living. I didn't rush the process. I wet his feet one at a time, rubbed them tenderly, rinsed them, and dried them off. I told him,

> We need more of this. Maybe it starts with us in the church. Regardless of our history, what if we started loving each other and serving each other? What if all of us humbled ourselves and said to you, 'I value you. I care what happens to you. I care what you experience in America. I care about the hurts and wounds of your past. I care about the history of my race against your race, and I'm sorry. I repent. I didn't enslave and oppress your people myself, but I take responsibility for my own race. Jesus didn't hurt anyone, but He took responsibility to provide healing for the hurts others caused. He took responsibility when He went to the cross, and I need to go back to the cross myself. We need healing in our relationship so we can be one together. You represent people who don't feel valued, and I want you to know that I'm committing my life to value you. I want you to grow up in an America where there are people of another race who value you. I love you.

When the video of this was posted on YouTube, it went viral. Many of the comments were very affirming and encouraging, but some were scathing. Some people who posted were obviously white, and some were obviously black. Some were thoughtful, and some were unintelligible. Among the protest posts were these: "This is a straight-up insult! Racial issues should not be preached from the pulpit." "This is weird and gross." "Sorry but as a black man this creeped me out."[22] Some people threatened me and said things I'm not going to put in this book! At that moment, I realized that I was just getting a little taste of what Jesus must have felt when He was mocked, beaten, and nailed to a cross for trying to reconcile people to God. As I look back on the responses to the video, I also realize that whenever you try to do something to bring reconciliation and healing into an area of deep hurt and anger, you're taking a risk. Over the years, I've seen many of my friends start to take risks in this area, and when they say something unpopular, their friends cancel them from the discussion. It's interesting: When the news feed shows racial injustice, people cry out for someone to speak up, but when someone does, they cry out for them to shut up! It often feels like a no-win situation, but as a Christian, I had to ignore the caustic comments and do what's right!

22. "A white man washing a black man's feet. VERY TOUCHING," YouTube, April 2, 2017, *https://www.youtube.com/watch?v=Mtu5mYJTKJ0*

Some would argue that I went too far by repenting of the sins of my race when I washed the black man's feet. No, I'm not a slave owner and I've never been one, but my people were, and they're not here. White people who are racist are outraged when I make this confession; intolerant whites aren't far behind. Those who prefer their own race are either annoyed or mystified that I believe repentance for historic sins is important, while those who are paternalistic feel "white guilt" and assume their painful feelings are the same as repentance, but people who are genuinely committed to racial reconciliation realize it takes this kind of heart to put some boards together to build a bridge between the races. And black people almost universally are amazed and grateful that a white person has acknowledged the injustices perpetrated on them for so many generations. This is just one way to address the offenses we've caused. I can handle the offenses that come back at me for taking this stand.

Perpetual Forgiveness

When we take offense, we stop the flow of God's love from us toward others. Sure, people may hurt our feelings, but we have a choice: to let it fester into resentment or "forgive as quickly and completely as the Master forgave you."

If anyone ever had good reason to take offense, it was Jesus. He was ridiculed and called names by the religious leaders. One of His own close followers betrayed Him into the hands of those who wanted to kill Him, and another denied even knowing Him. He was mocked in a kangaroo trial and condemned to death by the two social institutions designed to uphold justice—the government and the faith leaders. He was brutally whipped and nailed to boards. His response? "Father, forgive them, for they don't know what they're doing." Jesus looked beneath their cruelty and saw that they were misguided. Their deeds were evil, but His request for their forgiveness probably resonated with them for the rest of their lives. Who in the world does that? Jesus does ... and those who have been melted and molded by Jesus' love do it, too.

The emotional, spiritual, and relational watershed for us is forgiveness. We can let offenses multiply until our hearts are hard and bitter, or we can live in a perpetual state of forgiveness—looking beneath the surface to see that even racists are created in the image of God. If we see them this way, we'll be quick (or quicker) to forgive them. Isn't that exactly what Jesus did for us? He could have written us off as incorrigible and hopeless, but He loved us so much that He didn't turn and walk away. He kept loving us.

Forgiveness is one of the hardest things we ever do because it flies in the face of our instincts. Author Philip Yancey called forgiveness "the unnatural act," and he's right. We want justice, we want revenge, we want people to suffer at least as much as we do. But this leads only to our own heartache. Pastor and author Lewis Smedes had this insight: "Vengeance is having a videotape planted in your soul that cannot be turned off. It plays the painful scene over and over again inside your mind ... And each time it plays you feel the clap of pain again ... Forgiving turns off the videotape of pained memory. Forgiving sets you free."[23] And pastor Frederick Buechner explains how resentment is ultimately self-destructive: "Of the Seven Deadly Sins, anger is possibly the most fun. To lick your wounds, to smack your lips over grievances long past, to roll over your tongue the prospect of bitter confrontations still to come, to savor to the last toothsome morsel both the pain you are given and the pain you are giving back—in many ways it is a feast fit for a

23. Lewis Smedes, "Forgiveness: The Power to Change The Past," *Christianity Today*, January 7, 1983.

king. The chief drawback is that what you are wolfing down is yourself. The skeleton at the feast is you!"[24]

In an instant, we can make the choice to forgive, but don't be surprised that the feelings of hurt, loss, and anger last a while. God uses the process of grief to heal and strengthen us. Many people harbor offenses for their entire lives because the hurt seems too big, or the offenders aren't sorry, and they'll probably do it again. But the longer we delay our choice to forgive, the easier it is to say, "Oh, it's no big deal. I'm over it." But it *is* a big deal, and we're not over it until we address it in the presence of Jesus. For your sake, choose to forgive. For the other person's sake, choose to forgive, so there's an opportunity to mend the relationship. And for God's sake, choose to forgive because it makes you shine like a star with the light of His love.

Keep Loving

When a light shines on injustice and inequality, people have very strong emotional reactions. The victims of mistreatment—especially by authorities like the police and political leaders—often overreact with inflammatory language, with demands that may go far beyond

---

24. Frederick Buechner, *Wishful Thinking*, (San Francisco: Harper San Francisco, 1993), p. 2.

rectifying the actual offenses, and sometimes with violence. And of course, those who are committed to the status quo overreact to this overreaction, feeling completely justified in ignoring the genuine injustice because of the over-the-top reaction by the victims. We see this destructive dance played out in the news every time there's alleged police misconduct, immigrants are demonized, and the disadvantaged are overlooked.

It's very easy to get caught up in these reactions and forget who we are. We're not primarily Republicans or Democrats with an ax to grind on one end of the political divide or the other—we're people who have been rescued from sin and death by Jesus. Are we secure enough in God's love to be objective about the "war of words"? Can we love victims who have explosive emotions and who demand instant and sweeping change? Can we love those who are quick to despise the victims and write them off? Are we perceived as friends of both but wise enough to look for real answers to nagging questions?

This is our challenge, and this is our calling: to keep loving people even when their emotions have gotten the best of them. We're around these people every day.

The Measure of Love

Several years ago, I heard a man make a statement that rocked my world. He said, "Your love for God can be measured by the person you love the least." To back up his point, he turned to a passage in the Bible: "We love because he first loved us. Whoever claims to love God yet hates a brother or sister is a liar. For whoever does not love their brother or sister, whom they have seen cannot love God, whom they have not seen. And he has given us this command: Anyone who loves God must also love their brother and sister" (1 John 4: 19-21).

We usually assume our love quotient is shown by our kindness to our family and friends (assuming they're not our enemies, but who knows?). Who gives you the creeps? Who, when you hear their name, makes you grit your teeth? Who are the people you avoid? Who are the ones you criticize, either to their faces, in gossip with a friend, or anonymously online?

Can we love people who don't love us, who have nothing to give us, and who are genuinely offensive? A few years ago, my wife Colleen walked into a beauty shop to purchase hair products. (That's as far as I go in knowing what actually happens in those stores.) Colleen had difficulty getting any assistance from the attendant, a young black woman, even though no one else was in the store. The woman wouldn't give eye contact, and she gave curt answers to Colleen's questions. A few minutes later, a black lady walked in, and the attendant's demeanor completely changed. She was attentive, pleasant, and helpful toward the woman of her own race.

It became obvious to Colleen that she was being treated with disdain because of the color of her skin. In that moment, Colleen realized she had a choice: She could let her observation fuel her anger and storm out the door, or she could see this as an opportunity to love like Jesus loves. The Lord gave her the insight that the attendant almost certainly had experienced pain at the hands of white people. If Colleen had walked out, it would've only confirmed the girl's prejudices, but if she stayed, she had a chance to give her a very different experience with a white person. She thought, *It's not about the experience she's giving me; it's more about the experience I'm to give to her. I can be loving toward her even if she's being difficult toward me.* Colleen stayed, was very pleasant, and did her best to engage the woman in conversation. After she made her purchase, she thanked the attendant and left. Was it life changing for the attendant? Maybe not, but at least it took one stone off the pile of resentments she'd accumulated over many years in her interactions with white people.

Those we encounter each day may have a number of reasons for their negative attitudes toward people of other races. Prejudice and preference have been modeled by their families and reinforced by their friends, but they're also shaped by painful experiences. Our role now is to give people better experiences, to subtract some pain and add some kindness. We may not see a remarkable change because many more positive encounters may be necessary for the person to move to the positive side of the ledger, but our acts of love may be the turning point. Either way, it's what Jesus would do. It's what Jesus did. Love conquers all.

Think About It:

What are some signs of a supernaturally changed heart (not just a morally restrained heart)?

What is the legitimate role of government in social policy and race relations? What are its limitations?

How do you usually respond when you've been offended?

What do you think it means to "live in a perpetual state of forgiveness"? Is that attractive to you? Is it even possible?

Whose name makes you cringe? Who do you avoid? What do your answers say about the measure of your love for God?

What is one thing you can do today to show love toward someone you might normally overlook, or maybe, ignore?

chapter 5

Equal?

As a nation, we began by declaring that "all men are created equal." We now practically read it "all men are created equal, except negroes." When the Know-Nothings get control, it will read "all men are created equal, except negroes, and foreigners, and Catholics." When it comes to this I should prefer emigrating to some country where they make no pretense of loving liberty—to Russia, for instance, where despotism can be taken pure, and without the base alloy of hypocrisy. —Abraham Lincoln

To MOVE BEYOND preference and paternalism, we must see people as equals. Superiority of any kind, even if it motivates us to give generously to cross-cultural causes, still leaves a barrier between us and them. And it works both ways. Because of our history in America, and especially in the South, many whites assume they're superior, but blacks, Hispanics, Asians, and Native Americans can look at white people and sneer, "At least we're not bigots like they are!" Which, of course, makes them bigots, too.

Equality is the bedrock of racial reconciliation, and it's a much harder hill to climb than it may first appear.

When we launched our church in 1990, our part of the city was predominantly white, so the people who came were mostly white. I often preached on race and equality, and gradually, more people of color began to come. By the seventh year, a snapshot of our crowd showed that we were fairly balanced in our racial makeup. At that point, we asked a very gifted Jamaican woman to be one of our worship leaders, and the decision to put her in front opened the floodgates for other people of color to start coming to Victory. We began to see an influx of African Americans and other people of color attend our church. They came because they saw a familiar face on the stage, and many told me they were deeply encouraged (and very surprised) to hear a white pastor advocate for love, respect, and equality among the races. They realized this wasn't empty rhetoric, and they wanted to be part of something they'd had faint hopes would happen for many years.

Soon, the mix of races was no longer balanced. It didn't matter much in the worship service, but a problem arose in our children's ministry. Young white couples with small children became uncomfortable dropping their kids off. There were multiple issues: Some of our teachers were African women—African, not African American. They were first generation immigrants from Nigeria, Kenya, and other countries. In their cultures, mothers and teachers talked more authoritatively to children, but white parents saw it as inappropriately aggressive. They were used to black women in the South being deferential and polite. White parents, especially of younger kids, tend to be a bit overly protective, and many of them concluded that their children weren't safe—or at least, as safe as they'd like. And now, white kids were in the minority in these classes.

I can easily imagine the conversations among these parents. Very few of them talked to me about their concerns. Instead, they began "trying out" other churches where they felt more comfortable with the children's ministries— churches that were mostly white. A significant number of these families liked what they saw, and they left our church.

Actually, I see their point. I treasure my children too, and I want them to have the very best possible experience in church. But in my opinion, the best experience includes more than a Bible story, fun crafts, and a cookie. It includes learning to follow Christ in a diverse community of faith. I wish more of the white parents had come to me, and I wish their solution had been to get involved in the children's ministry to provide leadership and balance. But they didn't. At least, most of them didn't. After this, we sat down with our teachers and explained the challenges we were experiencing with the white parents. I was very encouraged to see them respond in love. They were more than willing to be sensitive to the white children who were now the minority in children's church. We got more involved, and we had fantastic conversations with Lauren to help her learn the value of diversity. The experience made her wiser, stronger, and more loving toward people of color. Lauren told us later how thankful she was that we allowed her to experience diversity and the challenges it brought with it.

For years, I followed many of the couples after they left our church. They had been very involved in leadership and as volunteers, and some had been close friends. They had been a big part of Victory, but after months and even years in other churches, very few of them participated in the lives of those churches. They had engaged very strongly at Victory, but they were quite disengaged in their new church homes. Sadly, some of them have never found church homes. They've drifted from one church to another, never quite satisfied, never giving themselves in service, never trusting God to use them like He did when they were with us. I've learned that this isn't rare. When families leave a church, a significant percentage drift like a boat without an anchor—slowly but surely moved by the wind and waves of culture. Maybe the ones who left us were so deeply disappointed in their experiences at Victory that they couldn't bring themselves to fully engage anywhere else. Or, maybe it was just easier to drift.

This was the season Victory actually became less diverse. When the white families left, each one consisted of parents and children, but when black and Hispanic families came, they brought their parents, brothers, sisters, nephews, nieces, uncles, aunts, and neighbors. It was a time of rapid growth. This phenomenon shows the difference in how people of different cultures connect with their families. If you have a history of experiencing prejudice, the tendency is to make your family your support system. You need each other for comfort and encouragement to deal with the disappointments as you live each day in a world that doesn't seem fair. When members of a family find a church that validates them, they want everybody else in the family to experience this love, too. However, most white families don't live under a cloud of racial prejudice, so their need for family support isn't as strong. They tend to lead more independent lives than black and Hispanic families, so they aren't as likely to bring their extended family to church.

Different Views

In thousands of conversations over the years, especially after young black men have been killed by police, race riots, and white nationalist marches, I've noticed two distinct perspectives in the minds and hearts of people. White people usually see racist language and behavior as an individual's sin—that *person* has a problem. People of color usually see racism as an ingrained *institutional* flaw (thus the term *systemic racism*). It's produced and prolonged by overt but mostly covert racism in laws, policies, politics, courts, law enforcement, schools, the criminal justice system, and every other aspect of our culture. They believe specific acts of racism are the bitter fruit from a tree with very deep roots, and it's not enough to focus on one piece of fruit. Of course, they believe the institutions are led by white people, with only a few flecks of color, so in their eyes the entire white race is culpable for the problem.

It's hard to argue that racial bias doesn't exist in our institutions. An article in *US News & World Report* gives alarming statistics:

• Black kids in preschool make up 18% of the school population but account for almost half of the out-of-school suspensions.

• Before graduating from high school, black children are three times more likely to be suspended, and almost seven in ten students referred to the police by school officials are black or Hispanic.

• In the juvenile justice system, black children are 18 times more likely than whites to be sentenced as adults, and they make up almost 60% of the children in juvenile detention.

• Black men are three times more likely to be searched at a traffic stop and six times more likely to go to jail. The Sentencing Project found that the reason for the disparity isn't that blacks are more prone to criminal acts, but there is "an implicit racial association of black Americans with dangerous or aggressive behavior."

• Before "Stop and Frisk" was eliminated in New York City, blacks were three times more likely than whites to be stopped and frisked, and Hispanics were four times more likely.

- A black convicted of murdering a white is twice as likely to receive the death penalty as a white who has murdered a black.

- 77% of those executed killed a white person, but only 13% killed a black person.

- For those fortunate enough to attend and graduate from college, black grads are twice as likely as whites to struggle to find employment.

- Overall, the jobless rate for blacks is twice that of whites. People with "black-sounding names" had to send out 50% more applications than those who have "white-sounding names."

- 73% of whites own their homes compared to 43% of blacks.[25]

Healthcare has always been a problem for the poor, and especially for people of color who are poor. Statistics show that a black boy born in a number of Southern states has a shorter life expectancy than a boy born in Bangladesh.[26] And in the COVID-19 pandemic, blacks are dying at more than twice the rate of whites. Some

25. "Institutional Racism Is Our Way of Life," Jeff Nesbit, *U.S. News and World Report*, May 6, 2015, *https://www.usnews.com/news/blogs/at-the-edge/2015/05/06/institutional-racism-is-our-way-of-life*

26. "State-Level Variations in Racial Disparities in Life Expectancy," NIH, *https://www.ncbi.nlm.nih.gov/pmc/articles/PMC3393007/*

of the disparity is due to the fact that many blacks and Hispanics are deemed "essential" workers in hospitals, meatpacking plants, and other jobs that put them at higher risk for the virus, but inequality in health has been a consistent fact in our country. Black children have twice the rate of infant mortality as whites, and black women are more than twice as likely to die in pregnancy or during childbirth. Shortly before he was assassinated in 1968, Robert Kennedy observed, "This is the violence of institutions; indifference and inaction and slow decay. This is the violence that afflicts the poor, that poisons relations between men because their skin has different colors. This is a slow destruction of a child by hunger, and schools without books and homes without heat."[27]

In an interview with Nicholas Kristof, Michelle A. Williams, Dean of the Harvard School of Public Health, stated, "That reality is palpable not just in the scourge of police violence that disproportionately kills black Americans, but in the vestiges of slavery and segregation that have permeated the social determinants of health. Racism has robbed

27. "Remarks to the Cleveland City Club, April 5, 1968," Robert F. Kennedy Papers, *https://www.jfklibrary.org/learn/about-jfk/the-kennedy-family/robert-f-kennedy/robert-f-kennedy-speeches/remarks-to-the-cleveland-city-club-april-5-1968*

black Americans from benefiting from the advancements they've fought for, bled for and died for throughout history. That reality manifests in myriad ways—from underfunded schools to the gutting of healthcare and social programs, to financial redlining, to mass incarceration, to voter suppression, to police brutality and more. And it is undeniably harming health and prematurely ending black lives."[28]

A study by the Centers for Disease Control found that poverty has had a direct effect on health outcomes before and during the pandemic. Relatively wealthy people have better diets, housing, and work conditions, and they have lower levels of stress. The poor have significantly higher rates of diabetes, obesity, asthma, hypertension, kidney disease, and pulmonary disease. Low-income neighborhoods have higher populations of people of color. The correlation of health with factors such as income and race has gotten worse in recent years as the gap between rich and poor has widened. Frederick Zimmerman, the author of a UCLA study, concluded, "What we now know about population health is that it is determined largely by social and economic policy factors. Because our current policy environment

28. "What If There Were No George Floyd Video?" Nicholas Kristof, *New York Times*, June 6, 2020, *https://www.nytimes.com/2020/06/06/opinion/sunday/george-floyd-structural-racism.html*

works best for those with social and economic power, it is no surprise that the outcomes of this process, including health outcomes, favor those with power. Those with less power, who are outside of the decision-making process, have been squeezed and their health has suffered."[29]

I've already addressed the income inequality and the disparity in household wealth. Some whites write all this off: "It's their own fault," "If they tried harder, they'd be more successful," "If they made better decisions, they'd stay out of trouble," or "It's no better than I'd expect." Certainly, all whites aren't racists, but more are intolerant, and many more show preference and are unwilling to take a hard look at the way our culture is stacked against black and brown people. I'm not excusing irresponsible and criminal behavior; I'm only saying that the deficits of equality in our country are very real. At least we should have more understanding and compassion for those who have to navigate all the land mines.

Black and brown people are well aware of the systemic obstacles in our society. They live in it every day. They're

29. "Who Is Most Likely to Die From the Coronavirus?" Yarna Serkez, *New York Times*, June 4, 2020, *https://www.nytimes.com/ interactive/2020/06/04/opinion/coronavirus-health-race-inequality. html?action=click&module=Opinion&pgtype=Homepage*

right to call out injustice, but they need to avoid painting all white people as members of the Klan who are out to get them. As they deal with the realities of institutional bias, they need to be open to connections with whites who are *for* them—and I know a lot of whites who are.

But for the vast majority of white people, social justice requires much more than a smile. In her book, *White Fragility*, Robin DiAngelo comments: "To continue reproducing racial inequality, the system only needs for white people to be really nice and carry on—to smile at people of color, to go to lunch with them on occasion. To be clear, being nice is generally a better policy than being mean. But niceness does not bring racism to the table and will not keep it on the table when so many of us who are white want it off. Niceness does not break with white solidarity and white silence. In fact, naming racism is often seen as not nice, triggering white fragility."[30]

Starting Points

It's the nature of the human heart to compare how we stack up with others—individually, in some cohesive group, and as a race. For instance, when I'm with pastors, I hear them talk about the size of their churches and how many "likes"

---

30. Robin DiAngelo, *White Fragility* (Boston: Beacon Press, 2018), p. 153.

they're getting on social media. Artists don't care about the size of churches; they compare their work—and their fame and the sales price of their work—to other artists. Engineers compare themselves to other engineers, CEOs to CEOs, plumbers to plumbers, and writers to writers. Comparison is standard equipment in every heart that necessarily produces superiority and inferiority, pride and shame.

A hard, unregenerate heart is the fertile soil of racism. A believing but immature heart allows intolerance and condones distrust. Until our hearts are changed, we don't just tolerate our sense of superiority over others—we relish it! People who hold these perspectives don't understand how God views people, and far too often, they don't even care. Until our hearts are softened by God's love, we won't see others as more important than ourselves, and we won't love them the way Jesus loves them.

But like a fish that doesn't comprehend that water is wet, most of us aren't aware of how much and how deeply comparison shapes our lives. In response, some of us try to intimidate people to have control over them, some of us feel compelled to fix others' problems so they'll appreciate us, some try very hard to be nice so others will be nice to them, and others spend their lives "hiding in plain sight" to avoid any threat of rejection or failure. These deeply embedded reactions shape every goal and every relationship. It's only when our hearts are changed by the grace of God that we stop comparing and controlling and begin to actually love people. After we're reconciled to God, we have the motivation, security, and power to take steps to reconcile with people.

Being nice to people to prove that we're good is only using them for our benefit. Offering pronouncements of love without a heart change makes our words inauthentic and repulsive—especially to the people we claim to love. As we've seen, true change happens only when God reveals a person's true nature of helplessness and hopelessness apart from Him. At that point, we no longer rely on how decent and competent we are, we no longer trust that our goodness is enough to win God's approval, and we no longer think being a better person than someone else gives us status with God. Instead, we face the fact that we have nothing—absolutely nothing—to impress God. Our hands are empty, but we look to the cross where Jesus paid the penalty of our sin. He took the punishment we deserve, so we can receive the honor He deserves. A heart that is thrilled to be forgiven and adored is then willing to forgive and love others, not to prove itself but to express its immense gratitude. When we're overwhelmed with the fact that we're fabulously rich in God's love, we'll be generous in sharing that love with others. A transformed heart inevitably moves us to love those we may have previously considered unlovable. It may take some time for us to move toward inclusion, but with every new insight and every clear choice, we'll take steps in that direction.

The Bible says that at the moment we trusted in Jesus, "God's love has been poured into our hearts through the Holy Spirit who has been given to us" (Romans 5:5, ESV), and that love begins to pour out of us in every relationship. At that point, we don't look at colors or classes of people—we see individuals, and we love them.

When our hearts are changed by God's grace, we'll make two crucial evaluations: All people have value, and loving people who are different from us isn't an option.

All people have inherent value.

We are people with opinions: We like this restaurant more than that one, we cheer for our team and not the other one, we like this hairstyle more than hers, we like our fishing spot more than his, and the list goes on to infinity. We intuitively rank virtually everything, so it's no surprise that we rank the value of people based on whatever criteria we choose.

However, a kingdom perspective is higher, richer, deeper—and much more challenging. In the first book of the Bible, God says that we are created in His image (Genesis 9:6). What does that mean? Decades ago in *All in the Family*, Archie Bunker reflected on this truth and announced, "God looks like me!" I think it's safe to say that's not it. There are some characteristics of God that He imparts to human beings, and some He reserves only for himself. Like Him, we're eternal and will live forever, we have a sense of justice, and we have the capacity for love, goodness, mercy, and purpose. But we're not omnipotent, omniscient, or omnipresent, and we're not sovereign over all things. And of course, even the traits that we share with God are badly tarnished in us.

But it's not just *us* who are created in the image of God ... it's also *them*. Conservatives believe in people getting what they deserve. What does the Bible say they deserve? Each person, from an unborn child to the most brilliant and gifted person to an incoherent senior, no matter what country or color, is more valuable than gold, oil, real estate, diamonds, and everything else we hold as precious. When you look in the mirror, that statement is true. When you see a homeless person on the street, it's true. When you see a fabulously wealthy hedge fund manager or a man cutting grass for a living, it's true. No one is outside this incredibly positive evaluation.

Who believes this? In one sense, we all do. In his letter to the Romans, Paul explained that even godless people who gaze at creation have some sense that God has made "his eternal power and divine nature" understandable (Romans 1:19-20). And later in the letter, he tells them that "When outsiders who have never heard of God's law follow it more or less by instinct, they confirm its truth by their obedience. They show that God's law is not something alien, imposed on us from without, but woven into the very fabric of our creation. There is something deep within them that echoes God's yes and no, right and wrong" (Romans 2:14-15, MSG). This truth and this law define the inherent dignity and worth of every person on the planet.

It's shocking to some but perfectly reasonable to others that unbelievers often have more concern for the poor, the marginalized, the incarcerated, and the sick than some Christians. Theologian D. A. Carson remarked, "Acts of kindness and self-sacrifice surface among every race and class of human beings, not because we are simple mixtures of good and evil, but because even in the midst of our deep rebellion, God restrains and displays his glory and goodness."[31] Instead of keeping a score sheet of who is acceptable and who isn't (especially who isn't), we should partner with unbelievers who have a heart for mercy and justice. We are all created in the image of a God who is merciful and just. Compassionate unbelievers are created in this image, and the people in need are created in this image. Believers have a message of grace that makes all this make much more sense, but many unbelievers have kind and generous hearts.

Our Savior was known for His immense sacrificial love for "those people"—outsiders and misfits. As we know Him better and follow Him more closely, we'll be known for our sacrificial love for the people overlooked or despised in our society. The designations of right and left, conservative and liberal, will sound silly and irrelevant. We'll live for a cause far more important than these.

You may want to jump out of your chair and ask, "Hey, are you saying irresponsible, harmful behavior doesn't matter?" Well, yes and no. Sin tarnishes the image of God in all of us, but it doesn't obliterate it. If Jesus values us so much

---

31. D. A. Carson, *Christ and Culture Revisited* (Grand Rapids: Eerdman's Publishing: 2012), p. 49.

that He left the glory and comfort of heaven to live for us and die in our place, surely we can walk across the street to show some kindness to someone in need. But irresponsible actions certainly matter. All around us, people are self-destructing with greed, bitterness, addictions, abuse, abandonment, foolish decisions about money, and many other bad choices. If we love them like Jesus loves them, we won't stand back, wag our fingers, and condemn them. We'll move toward them, assure them of God's forgiveness and purpose, and offer them a path forward. Some will take it; many won't. Our privilege and responsibility aren't to make them change but to offer a way out of the mess they've endured or created.

People are individuals.

It's easy to write off whole groups of people: White people are like this. Black people are like that. Hispanics and Asians always do this. Native Americans insist on that. Why do we use such blanket evaluations (and often, condemnations)? Because it makes our lives much easier. If we can label a whole class or race as unacceptable, we've effectively avoided any responsibility to get involved in their lives and go to the trouble to make nuanced observations. However, when we stop using universal labels, we can see people as individuals. Then we no longer see them as two-dimensional cardboard cutouts, but three-dimensional, complex human beings whose experiences and environments have shaped who they are today. Instead of discarding them as part of a group we don't particularly respect, we realize *that* man, *that* woman, *that* child is created in the image of God and of inestimable value.

Who is hard for you to love? For some of us, it's a person who hurt us in the past; for others it's a face we see every day. Jesus commanded us to love our enemies. They may be people who are actively trying to hurt us, those who just don't like us and gossip about us, or people who consider us so inconsequential that they don't give us the time of day. Jesus said to love them all. If we love only those who love us, it's a sign we haven't been changed from the inside out. In His most famous sermon, Jesus told the crowd,

> You're familiar with the old written law, "Love your friend," and its unwritten companion, "Hate your enemy." I'm challenging that. I'm telling you to love your enemies. Let them bring out the best in you, not the worst. When someone gives you a hard time, respond with the energies of prayer, for then you are working out of your true selves, your God-created selves. This is

what God does. He gives his best—the sun to warm and the rain to nourish—to everyone, regardless: the good and bad, the nice and nasty. If all you do is love the lovable, do you expect a bonus? Anybody can do that. If you simply say hello to those who greet you, do you expect a medal? Any run-of-the-mill sinner does that.

In a word, what I'm saying is, *Grow up*. You're kingdom subjects. Now live like it. Live out your God-created identity. Live generously and graciously toward others, the way God lives toward you. (Matthew 5:46-48, MSG)

As usual, Jesus turned things upside down.

Secrets, Rationalization, and Mercy

The Pharisees believed they were "better than." Better than the tax collectors who collaborated with the Roman occupiers to extract money from fellow Jews, better than the prostitutes who prowled the streets, better than the common people who hadn't had the opportunity to study the Bible or the additional rules the Pharisees added to it, better than the Sadducees whose political party was chummy with the Romans, and certainly better than the godless Roman officers and soldiers. To say the least, they were rigidly religious! They had laws about laws to be sure they didn't break any of them, and they were immensely proud of their righteousness. Jesus called them hypocrites because they claimed to follow God, but their hearts were far from Him. We can fall into the same pattern. We smile and look nice on Sunday morning, even if we've fought like caged cats on the way to church. We know the right things to say, and we know how to appear to have it all together. We can live behind masks to fool people, and we might even fool ourselves. It's spiritual poison.

I told our church,

Every one of us has broken the law at some point in our lives. In fact, many of us were guilty of speeding on the way to church this morning. (Nervous laughter.) We don't think it's a big deal. We've learned to tolerate a certain level of sin in our lives, but it always goes deeper than we want anyone to know. If you knew the dark side of my past before I came to Christ, you might have a very different perspective of me. You might not even come back to this church. Today, there are 2.3 million Americans behind bars in county jails and in state and federal prisons. The difference between them and me is that they got caught; I didn't. I could go down a list of offenses that got them arrested and convicted, and I could put a check mark next to many of them. Those are the ones I committed, too. Before you gasp, I'm quite sure many of you have done things you're not proud of. You've hurt people you were supposed to love, you've been selfish, used people, and done things you hope never make it into the light of day.

I let this sink in for a few seconds, and then I continued,

When I look at the people in prison, I see them the same way I see you—as men and women created in the image of God, of incredible value, and people Jesus Christ died to save. They did something wrong and are paying the price. All of us have done much more wrong toward God, but He paid the price for us. God doesn't have a caste system: some valuable, some not so much. Every single person is precious to Him.

I asked them to turn to a passage near the end of Matthew's account of the life of Jesus. At the end of time, Jesus will appear in a blaze of glory and will call people to give an account of their lives. In this passage, He gives us a vision of the future in a parable about a King and his subjects. He separates them into two groups, the ones on His right, the sheep, and those on His left, the goats.

Then the King will say to those on his right, "Enter, you who are blessed by my Father! Take what's coming to you in this kingdom. It's been ready for you since the world's foundation. And here's why:

I was hungry and you fed me,
I was thirsty and you gave me a drink,
I was homeless and you gave me a room,
I was shivering and you gave me clothes,
I was sick and you stopped to visit,
I was in prison and you came to me."

The people in that group are stunned. They responded, "Master, what are you talking about? When did we ever see you hungry and feed you, thirsty and give you a drink? And when did we ever see you sick or in prison and come to you?"

The King replied, "I'm telling the solemn truth: Whenever you did one of these things to someone overlooked or ignored, that was me—you did it to me."

Jesus' point is incredibly profound: When we care for people who are despised, overlooked, or forgotten, we're actually caring for Him! Let this sink in. When we move toward a person of another race, another socio-economic status, or another country, we're moving closer to Jesus. And when we truly love them by spending our time, expertise, and money to meet their needs, Jesus says He's the actual recipient of our affection. Amazing.

But the parable isn't over. The King turns to the other group, the ones on his left called goats, and tells them, "Get out, worthless goats! You're good for nothing but the fires of hell. And why? Because—

I was hungry and you gave me no meal,
I was thirsty and you gave me no drink,
I was homeless and you gave me no bed,
I was shivering and you gave me no clothes,
Sick and in prison, and you never visited."

These people are just as stunned as the other group, but not in a good way! They ask, "Master, what are you talking about? When did we ever see you hungry or thirsty or homeless or shivering or sick or in prison and didn't help?"

The King answers them, "I'm telling the solemn truth: Whenever you failed to do one of these things to someone who was being overlooked or ignored, that was me—you failed to do it to me."

The conclusion of the story is chilling:

Then those "goats" will be herded to their eternal doom, but the "sheep" to their eternal reward (Matthew 25:31-46, MSG).

Don't miss the point: The designation of sheep and goats wasn't because the sheep were flawless and the goats were evil. The King's evaluation was based on how they treated the disadvantaged. The King identified himself so strongly with the outcasts that he considered himself to be one of them, and how they were treated was how he considered himself to be treated.

So, how are you and I treating the hungry, the thirsty, the homeless, the naked, the sick, and the imprisoned? That's how Jesus considers that we treat Him.

We're prone to have categories of value instead of seeing every person as valuable, and we have lists of those who deserve love and those who don't. When Jesus said, "Do not judge, or you too will be judged" (Matthew 7:1), He didn't mean, "Don't make any evaluations." He meant, "When you evaluate, don't be harsh and condemning." He made evaluations all the time, and He wants us to make them about ourselves and about others, but our assessments shouldn't have two hard categories: "lovable" and "unlovable." They should give us insight about *how* to love each person. Certainly, we notice that some people are messing up their lives and harming others. Loving them doesn't mean we close our eyes to the truth, but that we point out their misbehavior and call them to be responsible—for their good more than for ours. We hold people accountable, so they'll see they can make better choices. That's *tough love*, but it's important that the second word is operative: love.

If we think we're "better than," the well of love will be bone dry, and we'll spend our lives condemning or avoiding those who don't measure up to our standards. It's easy for some of us to admit we're deeply flawed and in desperate need of God's amazing grace, but for some, it's much harder. They don't want to see their deep selfishness, jealousy, greed, and bitterness. They want others to see them as good and respectable, not broken and vulnerable. In *Just Mercy*, his book on the inequalities in the prison system, Bryan Stevenson comments:

We are all broken by something. We have all hurt someone and have been hurt. We all share the condition of
brokenness, even if our brokenness is not equivalent.
... Our shared vulnerability and imperfection nurtures
and sustains our capacity for compassion. We have a
choice. We can embrace our humanness, which means
embracing our broken natures and the compassion that
remains our best hope for healing. Or we can deny our
brokenness, foreswear compassion, and, as a result,
deny our own humanity.[32]

It's a spiritual truth: Our ability to love comes out of our
realization that we have no ability in ourselves to love others. The mercy we show is in proportion to the mercy we've
been given; our willingness to be involved in healing the
hurts of others comes out of our experience of the healing,
restoring love of God.

---

32. Bryan Stevenson, *Just Mercy* (New York: Random House, 2014), p. 271.

Think About It:

How would you describe the differences in how white people and people of color view injustice?

To what extent is human nature responsible for our selfishness and our views on race, and to what extent is our experience responsible? Explain your answer.

What are some specific, tangible signs that a person believes all people have inherent value? What are some signs he or she doesn't believe this?

Explain why it's important to see people as individuals instead of just part of a group.

How do you respond to Jesus' parable about the sheep and the goats? Any changes on the horizon?

chapter 6

Foundation Stones

When you say I want to talk about racial justice, that's not the same as saying I want to do something about racial justice. —Senator Marco Rubio

I'M THRILLED WITH the fact that we have progressives and conservatives in our church. To be sure, at times it would be a lot easier for our church to lean hard one way or the other. That would eliminate some conflict, but it would also prevent us from having rich and meaningful conversations about many very important things.

As I read articles, watch the news, and interact with people across the political spectrum, I've seen extreme polarization "up close and personal." Many of us live in echo chambers, feasting only on journalists and news outlets that reinforce what we already believe, and we're skeptical of the integrity (and the sanity) of those who disagree with us. Sociologists call this "confirmation bias." One expert described it this way:

When people would like a certain idea or concept to be true, they end up believing it to be true. They are motivated by wishful thinking. This error leads the individual to stop gathering information when the evidence gathered so far confirms the views or prejudices one would like to be true.

Once we have formed a view, we embrace information that confirms that view while ignoring, or rejecting, information that casts doubt on it. Confirmation bias suggests that we don't perceive circumstances objectively. We pick out those bits of data that make us feel good because they confirm our prejudices. Thus, we may become prisoners of our assumptions.[33]

People who view the world as dangerous are particularly susceptible to confirmation bias. Anxiety stimulates a fear response that heightens awareness (called hypervigilance) and causes them to be particularly reactive to perceived threats. This reaction is a lifesaver when a car swerves in front of us or our child is about to

---

33 "What Is Confirmation Bias?" Shahram Heshmat, Ph.D., *Psychology Today*, April 23, 2015, *https://www.psychologytoday.com/us/blog/science-choice/201504/what-is-confirmation-bias*

fall off the top of the slide, but it quickly subsides when the threat is over. However, the threat doesn't subside when we're obsessed with the Left taking our country from us or the Right caring only about people like them and increasing power and wealth. When we expose ourselves to one of these groups' incessant messages, fear multiplies, confirming every negative assumption about "those people" and making us seek protection and comfort from those who reinforce our fears. Confirmation bias has a snowball effect as fear makes us increasingly unwilling to listen to other points of view. This, of course, makes the people who disagree see us as rigid and demanding. This feeds their fears, which makes us even more suspicious of them, and the cycle intensifies.

Today, many Christians can't imagine anyone on the other side being a believer. For some Republicans, it's simply inconceivable that anyone who has a transformed heart could be a Democrat, and for some Democrats, it's equally unimaginable that someone who is truly born again could side with the Republicans. I've heard these arguments more times than I can count. Is there a better way to think about the problems in our culture than clinging to one side against the other?

Both

For thousands of years, the pillars of civilization have rested on two foundation stones: righteousness and justice. We see them throughout the Bible. For instance, the psalmist tells us, "Righteousness and justice are the foundations of [God's] throne" (Psalm 89:14, NKJV). When Isaiah was a prophet in Israel, the nation was threatened by the Assyrian army. The Jewish kings looked to other nations for protection, but Isaiah reminded them that the only one they could trust was God. They needed that reminder. They needed assurance. Through the prophet, God spoke to them:

> Look! I am placing a foundation stone in Jerusalem,
>   a firm and tested stone.
> It is a precious cornerstone that is safe to build on.
>   Whoever believes need never be shaken.
> I will test you with the measuring line of justice
>   and the plumb line of righteousness (Isaiah 28:16-
> 17, NLT).

Righteousness is *living right*—conforming to a moral code of conduct. In the Bible, we find clear, unambiguous directives for how we should live. The Ten Commandments is the most familiar of the lists, but there are many others. We see virtuous traits such as the list in Paul's letter to the Galatians: "But the fruit of the Spirit is love, joy, peace, forbearance, kindness, goodness, faithfulness, gentleness and self-control. Against such things there is no law" (Galatians 5:22-23), and in his letter to the Colossians:

> Therefore, as God's chosen people, holy and dearly loved, clothe yourselves with compassion, kindness, humility, gentleness and patience. Bear with each other and forgive one another if any of you has a grievance against someone. Forgive as the Lord forgave you. And over all these virtues put on love, which binds them all together in perfect unity (Colossians 3:12-14).

And of course, most people are familiar with Paul's list in his first letter to the Corinthians:

> Love is patient, love is kind. It does not envy, it does not boast, it is not proud. It does not dishonor others, it is not self-seeking, it is not easily angered, it keeps no record of wrongs. Love does not delight in evil but rejoices with the truth. It always protects, always trusts, always hopes, always perseveres (1 Corinthians 13:4-7).

But we also find lists of vices in Paul's letters, but even here, we find hope and comfort. In his corrective letter to the Corinthians, he wrote:

> Or do you not know that wrongdoers will not inherit the kingdom of God? Do not be deceived: Neither the sexually immoral nor idolaters nor adulterers nor men who have sex with men nor thieves nor the greedy nor drunkards nor slanderers nor swindlers will inherit the kingdom of God. And that is what some of you were. But you were washed, you were sanctified, you were justified in the name of the Lord Jesus Christ and by the Spirit of our God (1 Corinthians 6:9-11).

Righteousness (or unrighteousness) is shown in our integrity, generosity, kindness, and priorities of God first, people second, and anything else third.

Justice is *doing right,* especially correcting the injustices in society by defending the poor and marginalized and providing for those in need. We often think of justice only as punishing the guilty. It's certainly that, but in the Bible, we find people being excited that the king is coming to bring justice. Listen to the joy of the people who anticipated God's justice:

Let the heavens be glad, and the earth rejoice!
Let the sea and everything in it shout his praise!
Let the fields and their crops burst out with joy!
Let the trees of the forest sing for joy
before the LORD, for he is coming!
He is coming to judge the earth.
He will judge the world with justice,
and the nations with his truth. (Psalm 96:11-13)

To God, an important aspect of justice is bringing nourishment and protection to the poor, and it's righting all kinds of wrongs. That's why people were so thrilled to see the king show up!

Our two political parties have separated righteousness and justice, and each has taken up one as a badge of honor. Republicans tend to value righteousness. They're against same-sex marriage, abortion, climate change reforms, and immigration policies that are based on anything but strict adherence to the law (among other issues), and they're for religious liberties and gun rights (again, among many others). Democrats lean toward social justice. They're for immigration reform, but they would allow more legal immigration, the legalization of the DACA kids, and the admission of more political refugees. They aren't bothered very much by same-sex marriage, but they see the climate as an impending catastrophe, and they advocate forms of gun control. They're driving concern is to provide for the poor in the wealthiest country on earth—often at the expense of the rich. The gap between rich and poor doesn't concern Republicans very much because they believe everyone has equal opportunities, but the Democrats see the disparity as a sign that the country has lost its moral compass.

In short, Republicans insist on people living right, and Democrats insist on the power structures doing right to advance the interests of the poor—and the two parties talk past each other. Too often, the two foundation stones of civilization aren't seen as twin pillars of a strong society; each is seen as a problem to be demeaned and defeated by the other side.

The divide between righteousness and justice is plainly visible in churches. Some are all about righteousness—not God's but ours. They cry against addicts, broken families, undocumented immigrants, homosexuals, and other people who they say "are trying to take our country from us." But others have a heart for social justice and the poor, and they look down on Christians who don't seem to care about the disadvantaged. Their cry is against injustice in its many forms.

One of the most important steps in racial reconciliation is the commitment to understand the other side. One of my favorite quotes is from Stephen Covey's book, *The 7 Habits of Highly Effective People*. It's the key to all effective human relationships, and if you can master it, everything in your life will change. It's amazingly simple yet just as amazingly profound: "*Seek first to understand ... then to be understood.*"[34] When I talk to people who disagree with me, my goal is to engage long enough and deeply enough so that I understand the person's views almost as well as he does. If I can explain his perspective as well as he can, I've shown that I value him as a person and I'm open to his input. I may not change my mind about a particular issue, but at least we have a common bond of understanding. And quite often, when I see the issue more clearly, I realize nuances and options I hadn't seen before. The problem today is that almost everyone is focused exclusively on being understood, and they make far too little effort to understand.

---

34. Stephen R. Covey, *The 7 Habits of Highly Effective People* (New York: Simon & Schuster, 2013), p. 255.

Bubbles

I think it's safe to say that the vast majority of people in America—believers and unbelievers alike—live in either the righteousness bubble or the justice bubble. We don't even want to hear opposing views because understanding the other side might require us to change our perspectives, our hearts, our behavior ... and maybe our votes.

We need to be honest about how much we lean to one side. If we lean toward righteousness, we need to ask, "What are some genuine injustices that need to be remedied?" And if we lean toward justice, we need to ask, "How can I encourage people to be responsible citizens?"

The answer, though, isn't moderation. A grasp of God's righteousness and justice tempers those who are on the extremes, but it doesn't make them bland and tasteless. We need strong convictions, but convictions that are taken from the heart of God and the pages of Scripture, ones that aren't in either bubble. I would hope that people on the righteousness side can develop more compassion for those in need, and people on the justice side will realize that love isn't a license for people to do anything they want or for government to fix every problem. Living with this blend is harder than being on the extremes, but it's necessary if we're to have a loving, wise, powerful impact on our friends, our neighbors, and the country.

Let's look at the issue of immigration. On one side are people who believe immigrants are ruining our country. They complain that undocumented immigrants are putting a great strain on our agencies and healthcare, and they don't pay taxes. These critics overlook the fact that the vast majority of immigrants came here legally and are exceptionally hardworking men and women who came to America because they were desperate to earn enough money for their families to live on. Their work has a very practical value: A real estate developer said that without them, the average cost of a house in America would go up by $20,000. And they do pay taxes—over $11 billion each year. They pay sales tax, and when they pay their rent, their landlord pays city and county taxes out of it. I believe we could find an equitable, fair, and reasonable process to solve this problem, but it's much more politically expedient for those on the extremes to have this issue to attack and defend.

Statements by public figures inflame the animosity and spread misinformation. Consider these for instance:

• After a Mexican national won the New York marathon, a prominent conservative radio host remarked, "An immigration agent chased him for the last 10 miles." His listeners got a good laugh—at the expense of decency.

• A United States Representative warned, "I talked to a retired FBI agent who said that one of the things they were looking at were terrorist cells overseas who had figured out how to game our system. And it appeared they would have young women, who became pregnant, would get them into the United States to have a baby. ... And they would turn back where they could be raised and coddled as future terrorists." There is no evidence this has ever happened, but it planted suspicion in the minds of his constituents.

• A conservative commentator remarked, "Mexico has been overtaken by lawbreakers from bottom to top. And now, what [they're] protesting for is to have lawbreakers come here." Statistics show that the crime rate for immigrants, including illegals, is lower than the general population.

• A prominent government official stated flatly about undocumented immigrants, "These aren't people. These are animals."

• A U.S. Representative gave this advice: "What I'm talking about is the order of deportation, the sequence of deportation. It is almost impossible to move 11 million illegal immigrants overnight. You do it in steps."

These statements are the polar opposite of the policy that made our country a beacon of hope for the world. Our record, to be sure, is checkered, but we've welcomed millions of people who have come for a better life. Here are just a few statements from history:

• Emma Lazarus' beautiful poem is etched on the Statue of Liberty: "Give me your tired, your poor, your huddled masses yearning to breathe free, the wretched refuse of your teeming shore. Send these, the homeless, tempest-tost to me, I lift my lamp beside the golden door!"

• Benjamin Franklin, one of our nation's founders, noted, "Americans hailed newcomers to its shores as the bulwark of democracy, however, in times of crisis, it has also used the foreign born as a scapegoat for unsolved social problems."

• Former Secretary of Education, William Bennett, reflected, "We are all the sons or daughters of immigrants—some more recent than others—but all dedicated to the triumph of an idea that serves as the touchstone of what it means to be an American. This America is the only America that we have hitherto known—if being conservative has anything to do with conserving the principles of our past, then no conservative has any business bashing legal immigration."

• Republican Senator Spencer Abraham commented, "By balancing the needs of families and employers, and by extending a safe haven to those fleeing persecution, our immigration policy serves its historic purpose. Freedom and opportunity are the cornerstone of American society, and immigrants continue to embody that freedom."

A bumper sticker I want for my car says this: "Got a problem with immigration? Ask the Native Americans."

Real People, Real Stories

I've discovered one crucial factor that tempers a person's views on immigration: getting to know some immigrants. I'm a white man in a conservative part of a city in a very conservative state in the most conservative region of the country, but as I've gotten to know people who have come from other lands, stereotypes have melted away. I hear about where they've come from, why they've come, and their hopes and dreams. Personal relationships move me from seeing them as statistics and threats to viewing them as real people and friends.

I've also realized that I've lived a very sheltered life. I wouldn't have said that before I met these courageous people. I thought my life had been anything but sheltered. I'd experienced plenty of hard knocks, many of them self-inflicted, but nothing like these people have suffered.

If we only listen to the arch-conservative commentators, we'll believe people who are trying to come to our country are criminals, rapists, and drug dealers. A very few are, but the vast, vast majority are noble, wonderful men, women, and children who long for better lives. I've listened as they've told me about the oppressive conditions where they lived—the poverty and gang violence that threatened them and their children. The governments of their home countries are often broken and ineffective, providing little or no protection and precious few economic opportunities. They're looking for a safe place where they can earn a living and raise their families. When they show up at our border or at our airports, they've already demonstrated remarkable courage to chart a course for a better life for their families. They want to make America great.

Many Americans are afraid immigrants are going to recreate their home cultures within the borders of our nation, refusing to assimilate, not learning English, and not fully embracing our culture. Are many of them undocumented? Yes. Is that wrong? Yes. But we need to

put ourselves in their shoes. If you or I believed someone in our family might die of starvation, disease, or
violence, wouldn't we move heaven and earth to provide
a safe place to live? Yes, we would. Or at least I would.
And if we felt threatened with deportation, wouldn't we
try to be inconspicuous by living among our own people and making no attempts to assimilate? Of course.
But if I fled my home to a safer country, I'd learn the
language as fast as possible, and I'd adopt the new culture as my own. It would take time for me to adjust, but
I'd make every effort to respect the history, cuisine, and
habits of my new, adopted home. If I were from Korea,
I wouldn't move to Koreatown and interact only with
Koreans. Moving to another country is very hard and
requires many adjustments. We may want to keep the
values of the old and respect the new, but I would make
a commitment to lean hard toward the new.

And let's be clear, the images of crowds at the border
clamoring to get through have been created by our ineffective immigration policies. Most of the illegals in our
country, 68%, came in legally and overstayed their visas,
and the rest, 32%, crossed illegally. To the surprise of
many, Donald Kerwin, executive director of the Center

for Migration Studies, comments on his organization's study:

> It is clear from our research that persons who overstay their visas add to the U.S. undocumented population at a higher rate than border crossers. This is not a blip, but a trend which has become the norm. As these numbers indicate, construction of hundreds of more miles of border wall would not address the challenge of irregular migration into our country, far from it.

The study concludes,

> Since more than one-half of all U.S. undocumented residents arrive by air, visa-issuing posts have become the real frontline deterrent to undocumented migration. ... In another era, we would be celebrating our success.[35]

Many of the estimated 11 million undocumented immigrants have developed deep roots in America. A Pew Research Center study found that 66% have lived in the United States for more than 10 years. Surprisingly, only five states have seen the unauthorized immigrant population

---

35 "For 7th Consecutive Year, Visa Overstays Exceeded Illegal Border Crossings," Richard Gonzales, NPR, January 16, 2019, *https://www.npr.org/2019/01/16/686056668/for-seventh-consecutive-year-visa-overstays-exceeded-illegal-border-crossings*

increase in the past decade, and many others have seen a significant drop, including California with 775,000 fewer than 10 years ago.[36]

Law and Compassion

Yelling at each other from the right or the left is counter-productive. We need a reasonable approach with a workable process to solve the problem of illegal immigration. Those on the righteousness side say, "They broke the law. Send them back, and let them start over. They have to get in line with the others, and for them, it's the back of the line." The proponents of justice argue, "No, that's not only harsh, it's completely unworkable. Are we going to load up buses in every city and town in America and take them to their home countries? What will that do to families? And what kind of hole will that leave in construction, restaurants, and other businesses?"

A few years ago, the "Gang of Eight" senators from both parties met to find a solution, and they proposed a very workable process. However, it was shot down by the conservatives who believed it was too lenient. Since then, there has been virtually no bipartisan effort on

---

36. "5 facts about illegal immigration in the U.S." Jens Manuel Korgstad, Jeffrey S. Passel, and D'Vera Cohn, Pew Research Center, June 12, 2019, *https://www.pewresearch.org/fact-tank/2019/06/12/5-facts-about-illegal-immigration-in-the-u-s/*

immigration policy. I believe we need a strong blend of law and compassion. No one will be fully satisfied, but we need something we can live with. Some suggestions could include:

- A reconsidered policy of legal immigration.
- An offer of citizenship to kids and their parents who have been part of DACA.
- An end to family separation as a deterrent.
- A path to legalization for the roughly seven million who overstayed their visas, perhaps including a fine and a process to secure a green card.
- A path to legalization for the other four million who entered illegally, with a higher hill to climb, but not an insurmountable one.
- A guest-worker program that allows people to come to work and return home without fear of arrest, deportation, and a criminal record.
- An ongoing policy that respects the law and cares for people.

I don't expect calls from Washington asking me for advice, but if I got a call, that's what I'd say. There are, of course, many factors that shape the remedy to such a complicated issue, but we need to start somewhere.

Jerry Quiroz is a friend of mine who came to the United States illegally. He hired a "coyote" to get him into the country. When he lived in Mexico, he played professional soccer.

After being in America for a while, he met his wife Iliana, who supported him to pursue his dream of playing professional soccer in America. Jerry tried out and finally got a position on an American team. He was a playboy—a handsome and active athlete. Later, he was traded to a team in Atlanta, and he and Iliana started coming to our church. At Victory, he recommitted his life to Jesus because previously he had been living a double life. He heard us preach messages about the value of love in families. During this season, he had an encounter with Jesus and his heart toward his wife radically changed. They renewed their vows, and their relationship began to flourish.

While serving the children in their community as local missionaries, they received a fresh revelation of the love of God to care for orphans in a fatherless generation. With this new perspective, they decided to adopt. They now have two beautiful children, one of them with special needs, which required Iliana to quit her job to stay at home. We hired Jerry to be the director over our preschool ministry, and he has served with us for over 15 years. Who would have guessed that a playboy professional athlete would be changed by Jesus and have a heart for the youngest in our community of faith?

If we are to live with wisdom and strength, we must hold righteousness in one hand and justice in the other. Right living without caring for the disadvantaged makes us self-righteous, and caring without a commitment to integrity makes us sentimental but empty.

I hope everyone can see the importance of both of these aspects of culture, but to be honest, Christians have an advantage because righteousness and justice have been hand-in-glove throughout the history of our faith.

Recognize with way you lean, and begin to lean—at least a little—the other way.

Think About It:

How would you define and describe righteousness? And justice?

What are the consequences of separating them and focusing on one or the other?

How do you see confirmation bias in people you know? Do you think you're affected by it? Explain your answer.

Who "on the other side of the argument" is someone you respect and are willing to listen to? What difference would it make to really listen to opposing views?

In this chapter, I've used immigration as an example of how we can hold righteousness in one hand and justice in the other. How have you responded to the harsh rhetoric about immigrants by politicians, pastors, friends, and family members? How do you want to respond in the future?

What steps do you need to take to blend righteousness and justice in your perspective, your words, and your actions? What pushback do you expect? How will you respond?

chapter 7

Crazy Love

Racism is man's gravest threat to man—the maximum of hatred for a minimum of reason. —Abraham Heschel

JESUS WAS THE master of the art of asking penetrating questions, but occasionally, people asked Him questions. At one point, Jesus sent 70 people out to tell others about the kingdom of God. When they returned, they told wonderful stories of changed lives. A religious scholar was nearby, and he took this opportunity to ask Jesus a question—not because he wanted an answer, but because he was trying to trick Him to say something controversial. He asked, "Teacher, what do I need to do to get eternal life?"

Jesus answered the question with a question (which is a brilliant technique in teaching): "What is written in God's Law? How do you interpret it?"

The scholar responded from the wealth of his knowledge of the Bible: "That you love the Lord your God with all your passion and prayer and muscle and intelligence—and that you love your neighbor as well as you do yourself."

"Good answer!" said Jesus. "Do it and you'll live."

The conversation could have ended there, but it didn't. The man wanted to narrow the scope of the people God wanted him to love, so he asked, "And just how would you define 'neighbor'?"

That's the inherent question I've been asking throughout this book ... and throughout my career as a pastor: How narrowly or broadly do you and I define the scope of whom we love? Is it only those who are like us, who will return a favor, who contribute to our happiness, and who make us feel comfortable? Or is it wide enough to include people who don't meet our needs or make us happy?

Jesus launched into a story that must have stunned the scholar and the others who were listening. He told the story of the Good Samaritan. As you recall, the Jews despised Samaritans. In the story, Jesus shockingly made a Samaritan the hero. A Jewish man had been robbed, beaten, and left for dead on the side of the road. Two Jewish leaders, similar to a pastor and a deacon, walked by but didn't stop to help. They didn't want to get off their schedules, and they didn't want to get their hands dirty. They left the man in a heap beside the road. Then, a Samaritan walked up. He overcame deep-seated animosity between the races, and in fact, "When he saw the man's condition, his heart went out to him." He immediately went into EMS mode, disinfected and bandaged his wounds, put him on his donkey, and took him to an inn so he could convalesce. The next day, the Samaritan paid for the man's stay and promised to pay any additional charges when he returned from his trip.

That, Jesus was saying, is what love looks like. He asked the scholar, "What do you think? Which of the three became a neighbor to the man attacked by robbers?"

I'd love to see a replay of this scene. The scholar couldn't even bring himself to say the word "Samaritan." He replied, probably mumbling under his breath, "The one who treated him kindly."

Jesus surely smiled when He told him, "Go and do the same" (Luke 10:25-37).

When Jesus loved Samaritans, people thought He was insane. When He loved misfits and outcasts, they sneered at Him. When He loved a rich—but hated—tax collector, they assumed He had lost His way. That's the measure of His love: It's crazy!

A Wise Investment

As I've mentioned, one of the most important principles in any relationship, and especially in those that are strained in any way, is that it's more important to understand than to be understood. It's so important that we need to see the process as an investment in our relationship with the other person. When we invest in a stock, real estate, or anything else, we sacrifice in the short term to gain in the long term. Taking time to understand is a short-term sacrifice that can lead to long-term benefits in a relationship.

Conversations about race usually focus on political policies, but sometimes, they're about how each person interprets the past. Arguments flare up quickly, and ears get plugged by people insisting the other agree—or else! There's a better way. Let me give you some practical advice:

• *Leave your boxed set of convictions in another room.*

Quite often, we come to these conversations with a "package" of ironclad convictions, policy positions on every conceivable flashpoint we're willing to die for. We're spoiling for a fight and willing to take on all comers. That's not the way to begin a meaningful, bridge-building conversation. If we insist the other person agree with every point we hold, we create an environment for combat, not understanding.

- *The goal isn't to win.*

You may want to scream, "Are you kidding? That's absolutely the goal!" If that's what you're after, you'll marshal all your arguments, shoot your big guns, use every manipulative tool in your belt, and almost certainly harm the relationship. A better goal is to understand the other person, not to get him or her to cave under your barrage of "truth."

- *Be more like Jesus and ask great questions.*

Don't look for an opening to jump in to give your opinion and correct the foolish thinking of the other person. In fact, don't share your ideas and convictions at all for quite a while. You might say, "Tell me how you developed your perspective on this." And here's one for the ages: "Tell me more about that." If the person says, "What do you think?" you can say, "I'll tell you later, but right now I want to understand where you're coming from."

- *At some point, make sure the person knows you understand.*

You might say, "Let me tell you what I hear you saying." And explain the person's perspective with as much sympathy as you can muster. If you can do this, you'll be saying, "You're a reasonable person, and I value you even if I disagree." If you can't do this, you'll be saying, "You're a fool!"

• *Watch your tone of voice and your body language.*

A counselor once observed that in heated conversations, people tend to "get big" or "get little." Some of us lean forward, talk more loudly, glare at the person, and demand agreement. That's getting big. But in the same interaction, some seem to dissolve into nothingness. We can barely hear their voices, and they don't have an opinion ... about anything. That's getting little. Be a student of yourself. Take a few seconds periodically to notice what you look like and sound like. Are you getting big? Are you getting little? If you are, make the necessary corrections to be a mature, strong, wise person in the conversation.

• *If necessary, take time to cool off and then resume.*

If things get too tense, it's entirely appropriate to say, "I really want to understand what you're thinking, but we need to take a break. Let's pick it up again in an hour or so (or tomorrow, or whatever works) and see if we can make more progress without either of us getting upset."

• *There are times when you need to make declarative statements and let the chips fall.*

Most of what I'm suggesting is about listening, and listening even more, but sometimes we need to take a stand—not get big and try to intimidate people, but to calmly state what we believe. Before Donald Trump's election, Sarah Stewart Holland and Beth Silver wrote *I Think You're Wrong (But I'm Listening).* In an interview after the election, they said that navigating conversations about politics with family members had become more challenging since 2016. After the white supremacist rally in Charlottesville in 2017, some of their readers expected them to use their platform to advise people to try to understand the other side, but instead, Silvers wrote in a blog post: "In this moment, in this instance, I'm not willing to use [my platform] that way. My voice, my work is to say, 'That's wrong. That's unacceptable in America in 2017, and our businesses and politicians and families must say so in both words and actions.'"[37]

We can invest in understanding only if we're secure. If we're intimidated or defensive when people disagree with us, we won't have many meaningful dialogues. James, the half-brother of Jesus wrote in the opening of his letter to the first century Christians, "Everyone should be quick to listen,

37 "The Art of Navigating a Family Political Discussion, Peacefully," Ashley Fetters, *The Atlantic,* March 21, 2019, *https://www.theatlantic.com/family/archive/2019/03/can-families-communicate-across-the-political-divide/585379/*

slow to speak and slow to become angry" (James 1:19). His advice is always pertinent, and never more than now.

Lay Aside Your Rights

A lot of people attend church because they believe it's the right thing to do, because their families have always gone to church, and because they want to be part of the community. For many of them, their understanding of the faith is that Jesus has given them fire insurance, a "get out of hell card." They're right, but they're wrong. Yes, when we trust in Jesus, our eternal destiny changes. We had been headed for a place of utter darkness, where the worm does not die and the fire does not cease, but now we're bound for heaven. That's a glorious truth, but it's only one part of what it means to be a Christian. We were saved by the King, we were adopted by the Father, and we're now involved in the "family business" of redeeming every person who will listen to the gospel of grace. Being a Christian is far more than fire insurance; it's love for and loyalty to the One who rescued us. We've been set free from the penalty of sin, but we're now sons and daughters in a royal family, with incredible privileges and significant responsibilities. We're free *from* sin, and we're free *to* serve the God who loves us to death ... literally. One way to look at the experience of grace is to see that before we trusted Christ, we were exiles, living apart from Him, but God ". . . has rescued us from the dominion of darkness and brought us into the kingdom of the Son he loves, in whom we have redemption, the forgiveness of sins" (Colossians 1:13-14). We've changed passports: We were citizens of the domain of darkness, but now we're citizens of God's kingdom. Understanding our citizenship makes all the difference in how we respond in every situation.

This is a crucial distinction when we think about our rights. Our country has enshrined our values in The Bill of Rights, and one of the great seasons of our nation's history is the Civil Rights movement. People in other countries struggle to gain the right of free speech, the right to worship in the way they want, freedom of the press, freedom of assembly, the right to bear arms, and many others—but we take these for granted. In the 60s, these basic American rights were extended by law to every citizen, regardless of race, color, or creed. But as Christians, we give up our rights. If not, we're no different from every other American. When we insist on our rights, we aren't light in the darkness and salt that flavors and preserves. Let me explain.

Jesus was incredibly tender and compassionate, but He was also as fierce as a lion. He welcomed everyone, but the call to follow Him was a very high standard. He told His disciples:

> Whoever wants to be my disciple must deny themselves and take up their cross and follow me. For whoever wants to save their life will lose it, but whoever loses their life for me will find it. What good will it be for someone to gain the whole world, yet forfeit their soul? Or what can anyone give in exchange for their soul? (Matthew 16:24-26)

What does it mean to "deny" ourselves? It doesn't mean we hate ourselves or ignore our basic needs. It means we say "no" to our selfish desires, and we consider our role in the kingdom more important than our rights as Americans. How can we tell? If we know what to look for, we'll see it everywhere. When we say, "The Left is ruining our country," we're making a statement that it's our right to determine the direction of the country. When we say it may not be appropriate for U.S. military bases in the South to be named after Confederate leaders, some insist, "That's our heritage! You can't take that away from us!" That's a statement of perceived rights. Or when people react with riots and looting to the police killing a black man, they're saying, "We have the right to destroy things because we've been violated!"

Anger, frustration, and arrogance are natural human responses to injustice. We may feel these powerful emotions, but Christ wants us to give up our right of vengeance, our right to be offended, and our right to hold grudges. Instead, we follow Jesus in a life of grace and truth. There's nothing inherently wrong with the feeling of anger, but our expressions of anger are often sinful. Paul wrote, "In your anger do not sin" (Ephesians 4:26). In fact, it's totally inappropriate *not to* be angry at injustice! That's a lack of compassion for the people who have been violated. However, we need love and wisdom to temper our anger and propel our grief into helpful, healing actions. What does that look like?

As I write this chapter, yet another black man has died at the hands of a white policeman, this time in Minneapolis. A bystander took a video of the policeman's knee on the neck of George Floyd for almost nine long minutes. He called for his mother and gasped a dozen times, "I can't breathe," and we saw his lifeless body still held down by the policeman's knee. I asked some of the black pastors on our staff to share the heartache this scene brought up in them. As I called on Andrew Momon, he got choked up for two agonizing minutes, and then his wife Kendra described their ongoing pain and deep disappointment that this kind of racial brutality still goes on in the United States. She explained that the real threat is to black men, more than women, because many whites feel threatened by them—even the sight of them.

On the same day George Floyd died, a black man, Christian Cooper, was birdwatching in New York's Central Park and politely asked a white woman to put a leash on her dog in that section of the park. She immediately told him, "I'm taking a picture and calling the cops. I'm going to tell them there's an African American man threatening my life." Later, his sister shared his video of the event. She wrote, "I share this more [because] we see the narrative 'she called the police on a black man' like the man is some faceless, nameless idea, rather than a living, breathing person." The white woman was fired from her job because of the incident, but in an interview, Cooper calmly explained that he wished she hadn't been fired. For her, the sight of a black man, no matter how polite and benign (He was birdwatching!), was a terrible threat to her life. But for him, even her obvious overreaction and her threat to him didn't inflame a hint of bitterness.[38] Eventually, the woman apologized. In

38. "Christian Cooper Is My Brother. Here's Why I Posted His Video," Melody Cooper, *New York Times*, May 31, 2020, *https://www.nytimes.com/2020/05/31/opinion/chris-cooper-central-park.html*

an interview, Cooper was asked how he responded to her. He remarked,

> I do accept her apology. I think it's a first step. I think she's gotta do some reflection on what happened because up until the moment when she made that statement … it was just a conflict between a birder and a dog walker, and then she took it to a very dark place. I think she's gotta sort of examine why and how that happened. It's not really about her and her poor judgment in a snap second. It's about the underlying current of racism and racial perceptions that's been going on for centuries and that permeates this city and this country that she tapped into.[39]

Christian Cooper gave up his right to be offended. His calm demeanor during and after the altercation with the woman showed a depth of character I greatly admire. In "a nation of victims" where people feel completely justified to express outrage over every slight and offense, Cooper is a model of what it means to give up the right of vengeance.

---

39 "Christian Cooper accepts apology from woman at center of Central Park confrontation," Allie Yang, ABCNews, May 28, 2020, *https://abcnews.go.com/US/ christian-cooper-accepts-apology-woman-center-central-park/story?id=70926679*

I want to be clear, though, that for Christians to give up their rights doesn't mean we allow others to be cruel toward us. I can imagine how "give up our rights" sounds to a woman who is the victim of domestic violence or a child who lives with an abusive parent. We have the right of self-protection against this kind of treatment. Paul demonstrated this when he was about to be flogged but told the soldier that he was a Roman citizen with rights. Jesus defended himself in arguments with the religious leaders, and at least on some occasions, He escaped their grasp to live and love another day. But everything He said and did was for the Father's purposes, not to please himself. That's what it means to deny ourselves: We live for a purpose much higher and greater than our own purposes—we live for God's purposes.

Inevitably, people offend us—sometimes accidentally but often intentionally. When this happens, we have a choice to make: to hold onto our rights as victims and react by trying to make the person pay for what he or she did, or to give up our rights and respond in love—not caving in and rolling over passively, but living in that beautiful (and very rare) blend of truth and grace. If we react by claiming our right to be offended and defend ourselves, it will be throwing gas on the fire. The other person will get defensive, and the destructive cycle continues. But if we choose love, forgiveness, and kindness, the fire diminishes and the cycle of vengeance is broken, at least on our side.

But is that even possible?

The Watershed

It's human nature to prefer our own kind, to despise "the other," and to avoid interaction with people who don't contribute to our happiness. Jesus modeled and taught a kind of love that is a watershed in human history. In His greatest sermon, He spelled it out. He began by saying something they all readily understood: "You have heard that it was said, 'Love your neighbor and hate your enemy.'" I can imagine all of them nodding. That's what they had been taught all their lives. In fact, the saying, "an eye for an eye and a tooth for a tooth," the rule of *lex talionis*, was given to prevent people from going beyond proportional retribution. In other words, if someone gouged out one of your eyes, it prevented you from gouging out both of his (if you could find him). Equal reciprocity was as much grace and kindness as anyone could expect.

But Jesus gives an utterly astounding alternative: "But I say to you, love your enemies, bless those who curse you, do good to those who hate you, and pray for those who spitefully use you and persecute you" (Matthew 5:44, NKJV). Who were their enemies? The Jews were a proud people. God had given them a unique identity, a rich history, and the land of their fathers, but for the previous couple of centuries, the Syrians and Romans had occupied their land as conquerors. The vast majority of us don't have a good grasp of what it means to live in a homeland under foreign domination. For reference, we might look at the French, Belgians, and Poles when the German Nazis oppressed them during World War II. It was demoralizing and dehumanizing. For the Jews in Palestine in the first century, the Romans were like the Nazi occupying forces—and they hated them. And of course, there were Samaritans who lived only a few miles from Jerusalem. They, too, were sworn enemies of the Jews. During this period, a political party called the Zealots believed it was their destiny to lead a revolt against the Romans. One of Jesus' disciples was a Zealot, and it's possible that the two "thieves" on the cross next to Jesus were members of the group that advocated a violent overthrow of Roman authority. (We know them as thieves, but thieves weren't executed this way. The cross was reserved for the very worst criminals, especially traitors like the Zealots.) Shockingly, unimaginably, Jesus was telling His followers to love the Roman occupiers, pray for them, and bless them. He was telling them to give up their right to vengeance and replace it with genuine love. That's a tall order, isn't it?

This is what sets Christianity apart from all other belief systems, spiritual or secular. Notice that the people Jesus wants us to love aren't "out there somewhere." They're actively persecuting us and trying their best to harm us. They curse us and do what they can to destroy our reputations and our security. They may live in our neighborhoods, participate on our sports teams, work side by side with us every day, or live under our roofs. No one, Jesus is saying, is off limits to our love.

Jesus must have known people listening to Him that day would be utterly flabbergasted, so He made the connection to help them (and us) understand. When we love our enemies, pray for those who persecute us, and bless those who cruelly use us, we're like God. We need to remember that we were His enemies, we worshipped created things instead of the Creator, and we used people instead of loving them ... but the love of God is so great that He loved us still. That's the deep well of love we can draw from; we love others the way God loves us.

But Jesus wasn't quite through making His point. Lots of people talk about love, but it's not this kind of love they're referring to. Their brand is reciprocal, not sacrificial. He continued His message by asking questions with obvious answers: "If you love those who love you, what reward will you get? Are not even the tax collectors doing that? And if you greet only your own people, what are you doing more than others? Do not even pagans do that?" It's no big deal to love those who love us, but it's a really big deal to love people who have nothing to offer in return. They don't make our lives better, they don't make us more comfortable, and they don't care about us at all—but we love them still. Jesus ends this part of His message with the chilling instruction: "Be perfect as your heavenly Father is perfect" (Matthew 5:38-48). He's not talking about sinless perfection. He's referring to the incredible wealth of love—perfect love, not superficial or conditional—God has poured into our hearts, so we can pay it forward in the lives of people who aren't like us and don't like us.

Later in the first century when the church was growing by attracting people of all races and nationalities, there were some predictable suspicions and animosities. In his first letter to all the churches, John wrote: "Dear friends, let us love one another, for love comes from God. Everyone who loves has been born of God and knows God. Whoever does not love does not know God, because God is love. This is how God showed his love among us: He sent his one and only Son into the world that we might live through him. This is love: not that we loved God, but that he loved us and sent his Son as an atoning sacrifice for our sins. Dear friends, since God so loved us, we also ought to love one another" (1 John 4:7-11).

Did you get that? "Whoever does not love does not know God, because God is love." Here's the way I'd put it: People who genuinely know God have experienced such love that it flows from them to people they wouldn't naturally love. Whites, blacks, Hispanics, Asians, and Native Americans have built up animosity for centuries, but it melts away in the compassion, kindness, and affection we experience in Christ. Is this only among believers? Well, yes and no. It's especially true among those who know Jesus because we have a shared experience of being forgiven, loved, and accepted by the King of the universe. But as we overcome our natural racial tensions and demonstrate love for each other, the world will notice. It will be incredibly attractive to some and confusing to others, and some will be threatened because they can't comprehend anything so strange and wonderful.

The point is clear: We aren't expected to love from an empty heart. As our hearts are filled with God's amazing love, we can love others. But the converse is also clear: If we don't love others, it's a sign that the love of God hasn't yet penetrated our hearts.

A Different Lens

A few years ago, Colleen and I took a girl into our home. We discovered that she had been homeless before, and we felt God telling us to try and help her. She came from a mixed-race family: her father was African American, and her mother was Mexican. Her father had struggled with alcohol abuse and drug addiction, but for a season after she was born, he was able to climb the ladder, eventually owning his own business in a rural predominantly white community. Unfortunately, in an economic downturn, her father lost his business, and he quickly returned to the patterns that had led to previous periods of incarceration. For Khylee and her family, it turned into a season of financial uncertainty, moving in and out of temporary housing. Her father's addiction soon led to an arrest and prolonged conviction on drug-related charges driven by the "three strikes" law. During the final sentence, her father was born again and healed of his addiction. However, Khylee and her family didn't reap the benefits of his rehabilitation because he passed away 17 years later from cancer while he was still incarcerated. Khylee's mother was left to raise five children. Having little formal education, her mother endured the insurmountable pressures of doing that without a support system. After six years, Khylee's mother suffered a mental breakdown and left home, never to return.

For a while, the five kids found a way to make it on their own: attending school, playing sports, and working part-time jobs. They obviously needed help. Eventually, the oldest sibling found a place of his own. Khylee and the next oldest were taken in by families whose kids were on the same sports teams, and their younger siblings were sent to live with extended family in a different city. Until she went to college, Khylee moved from home to home of various friends and families in the community.

Khylee moved to Atlanta after graduating from college and came to our home several years later. She had been traumatized by her family experiences. We wanted to give her the love and security she desperately needed. Eventually, she became like our second daughter and now will always be a part of our family.

Years later, she joined the Army and was assigned a tour in Kuwait. The blacks and whites in her unit deployed to Thailand while she attended a leadership course. While deployed, the group saw it as an opportunity to break some rules and have a good time. When she learned about the issues and tried to report them, the group retaliated against Khylee. The tension between her and the others grew fierce, so she called Colleen and me to ask for our advice. She wanted to find a way to leave the unit, but I told her, "A person's level of disappointment is the difference between expectation and realization. Your disappointment is understandable because you expected to be in a mutually supportive unit, and it's not. As strange as it may sound, you need to lower your expectations to match the situation's reality. Then you'll be wise, you can be strong, and you won't be as disappointed. I'm not saying it'll be easy and fun, but it sure won't surprise you any longer."

The same principle is true in race relations. It's foolish for us to expect people who don't know Jesus to show love and compassion toward people who aren't like them. It's much more reasonable to expect people to think, feel, and act like Roman conquerors or Samaritans—or like the Jews who despised them. The Bible says clearly that those who don't know God are selfish, power-hungry, easily threatened, and reactive. When we expect those people to be kind and understanding, we're easily disappointed—and furious.

How did Jesus respond to people who ridiculed Him, slandered Him, and plotted to kill Him? He loved them. Again and again, He moved toward His enemies to engage them in conversation, to teach them about the kingdom of God, and demonstrate God's love to them. They didn't wait until the end to begin their plot to kill Him. In the third chapter of Mark's Gospel, we see Jesus in a synagogue healing a man who had a shriveled hand. You might think everyone would be thrilled, but the religious leaders were angry. "Then the Pharisees went out and began to plot with the Herodians how they might kill Jesus" (Mark 3:6). This is remarkable. The Pharisees were the party of tradition, the ones who taught the Bible and tried very hard to follow every command. The Herodians were the family of King Herod, a Jew who was a puppet of the Romans. The Pharisees and the Herodians detested each other, but they found common cause in their hatred of Jesus. Why? Because His kindness and His power to heal—and His popularity—threatened their place in the culture. Maybe this scene is where we get the notion that "No good deed goes unpunished." And as we've seen, when Jesus was on the cross, the innocent dying for the guilty, His haters kept pouring contempt on Him and mocking Him. He looked at their scowling faces and prayed, "Father, forgive them, for they do not know what they're doing" (Luke 23:34). "What?" we want to yell. "What do You mean they don't know what they're doing? Isn't it obvious they're killing You?" Yes, but that's not what Jesus meant. He was saying they truly believed what they were doing was good and right. They didn't understand their fear had blinded them and they were killing their Messiah, their King, the Lord of Life.

Jesus used a different lens to see the people who hated Him. He looked beneath the surface and into their hearts. They saw Him as a threat, but He was their healer. They saw Him as weak, but He was the all-powerful Creator. They saw Him as a rebel, but He was the only person who has ever been utterly faithful.

We need Jesus' lens. When I look at people who are prejudiced, either whites against people of color or people of color against whites, I try to look beneath the surface and realize they've been taught discrimination from the time they were little children. I'm not surprised they're racist, intolerant, or at best paternalistic, so I'm a realist when I hear their words and see their actions.

As I explained this perspective to Khylee, her anxiety subsided, and she had a new sense of confidence that she could handle the situation. She lowered her expectations, which made her less defensive, and she realized they had ridiculed her out of their own insecurities. She made a commitment to love them even if they don't love her in return, do good to them even if they want to harm her, and pray for them even though they say ugly things to her. The only way to conquer evil is with good. Responding to evil with more evil inflames both sides and makes the situation worse.

Loving "the other" is what real Christians do ... or it's at least what real Christians genuinely want to do. And, they will move heaven and earth to make it happen. People may think we're crazy if we love like this. That's what they thought about Jesus, so we're in good company.

Think About It:

Who do you know who is a good listener? What does that person do to understand people really well? What effect does he or she have on you?

Look at the communication principles in the section called "A Wise Investment." Which of these do you do pretty well? Which need some improvement? What are some specific steps you can take?

Do you agree or disagree with the concept that we Christians lay aside our rights when we choose to follow Jesus and "deny" ourselves? Explain your answer.

On a scale of 0 (not in the least) to 10 (all day every day), rate yourself on how well you love, pray for, and bless people who are "the other." What does this assessment tell you about yourself?

What are some excuses people (especially those who claim to be Christians) use when they refuse to love like Jesus loves?

How would learning to live by this statement help you? "A person's level of disappointment is the difference between expectation and realization."

chapter 8

Breaking Down Walls

God does His best work in the midst of unity. In fact, so
essential is the issue of oneness in the church that we are
told to be on guard against those who try to destroy it.
God has intentionally reconciled racially divided groups
into one new man, uniting them into a new body, in order
that the church can function as one. When the church
functions as one, we boldly brag on God to a world in
desperate need of experiencing Him. —Tony Evans

IN ISRAEL, THE wall between the Jewish people and
the Palestinians is unmistakable. It was begun in September of 2000 during the Second Intifada to stop Palestinian political violence and was finished three years
later. The 440-mile barrier was proposed as a temporary measure but is now seen as the permanent border
between Israel and the West Bank. Whatever we may
think about the justice or injustice of the two sides, the
point is that a physical barrier was erected to keep two

ethnic groups apart. And it has been remarkably successful.

Another visible, tangible wall existed many years earlier in the same area. The temple in Jerusalem, the most sacred site for Jews, had a number of clearly marked areas, including the holy of holies where only the high priest entered once a year, the altar for sacrifices, the court of the women, and the court of the Gentiles. The area designated for the Gentiles (all those who weren't Jewish but still wanted to worship God) was divided by a wall to keep the races separate. As we saw in Jesus' interaction with the Samaritan woman drawing water at the well, she was shocked that Jesus would approach her, "For Jews do not associate with Samaritans" (John 4:9).

The Jews had a long history of being God's "special possession," a status superior to every other nation and group in the world. A few years later, Paul used the imagery of the wall separating Gentiles in the temple to make a dramatic point. He wrote that all of us—Jew and Gentile—were in the same boat: alienated from God because of our darkened hearts. "But because of his great love for us, God, who is rich in mercy, made us alive with Christ even when we were dead in our transgressions—it is by grace you have been saved" (Ephesians 2:4-5).

But Paul made it crystal clear that things have changed: There are no distinctions in God's family—no insiders and outsiders, no higher or lower races, no value judgments based on background or customs. The Jews had enjoyed a favored status for centuries, but now the door was open to everyone. He addressed the Gentiles: "Remember that at that time you were separate from Christ, excluded from citizenship in Israel and foreigners to the covenants of the promise, without hope and without God in the world. But now in Christ Jesus you who once were far away have been brought near by the blood of Christ" (12-13).

The previous assumptions about racial superiority were shattered, the fear of rejection was dissolved, and the door to equality was open. Paul used the picture of the wall in the temple to make his point:

For he himself is our peace, who has made the two groups one and has destroyed the barrier, the dividing wall of hostility, by setting aside in his flesh the law with its commands and regulations. His purpose was to create in himself one new humanity out of the two, thus making peace, and in one body to reconcile both of them to God through the cross, by which he put to death their hostility. He came and preached peace to you who were far away and peace to those who were near. For through him we both have access to the Father by one Spirit. (14-18)

No difference? No difference. Ancient animosities put to rest? Yes, dissolved in the love of Jesus. No more separation? No more because grace has obliterated the dividing wall!

However, the wall doesn't come down by merely waving our hands. In the first century, unity required clear teaching and the courage to reach out to care for people who had been on the other side of the wall. For us, change begins when we identify the bricks.

Bricks in the Wall

History, culture, and natural suspicions are factors that keep walls high and strong. When we examine them closely, we'll see how they stay in place so well and so long.

• *Conflicting perspectives*

In any dramatic interracial event, it seems that the races view it from the perspectives of different planets. Whites localize the problem—it's that person's fault; but blacks globalize it—the issue is always much deeper and wider than the single circumstance. Whites often insist that blacks and Hispanics have plenty of opportunities, and any attempt to create balance is actually reverse discrimination against them. Blacks live with the devastation of decades of poverty, substandard education, distrust, and taunts. They see themselves as victims of the system, not with plenty of doors open to opportunities. Hispanics haven't had the same history, but many of them believe whites are against them.

• *Simplistic solutions*

Some who know my heart for reconciliation have told me, "If we all become colorblind, the racial tensions will go away." Well, that would be nice, but it's an unreasonable assumption. Some point to the welfare state created by Lyndon Johnson's Great Society as the national program that had good intentions but has had devastating unintended consequences in the lives of poor people, especially black families. Inequalities in housing, schools, employment, wages, and healthcare can't just be wished away.

"Just" is the wrong word to use when we talk about matters of race. Too many people say, "If black people would just (do this or that), they'd be fine, and they wouldn't complain so much." (And some of the ones who say that are black people.) But others insist, "If white people would just give us a chance, give us better schools, or help us get into colleges, we'd make real progress."

The problem of race relations has been with us since the first slaves were unloaded from a ship in Jamestown in 1619 and only seven years later on the docks of New York. We fought the long and bloody Civil War to end slavery, but blacks remained second-class citizens and lived in constant fear for almost 100 years after the last shots were fired. The scale of equality has been more balanced since the advances in the 60s, but we're not there yet. When a soldier gets PTSD in combat, the effects last for years, if not the person's entire life. Slavery and Jim Crow segregation are a type of PTSD in the black psyche, and the effects are still with them. We've taken steps forward since the Civil Rights Act of 1964, but the racial hatred we've seen in the past few years makes me wonder how much progress we've really made.

• *Distrust*

Whites who don't have any compassion for the problems in black America either don't know any black people or their hearts haven't been softened by the love of God. I don't wonder why blacks feel they have to force their way into the mainstream of America. They don't trust whites to have their backs because most of what they've seen, heard, and experienced consists of subtle or overt forms of rejection.

Hispanics have seen America as the land of opportunity to provide for their families, especially in contrast with the gang violence and poverty in their homelands. But the rhetoric of some conservatives is chilling to them. They feel maligned. As we've seen, most came to our country legally and overstayed their visas, but all of those who are here illegally feel incredibly vulnerable to the harsh language and proposals they hear from some in government—and in the church.

Actually, Hispanics often feel rejected by blacks, too, because blacks believe they are taking some of their opportunities. Among Hispanics, I've seen prejudice between people from different countries: For instance, Columbians (and people from most of the other Latin American countries) look down on Mexicans.

Many Asians are simply disinterested in racial reconciliation. They generally stay with their own people, creating subcultures where they shop, work, and live with people like them.

The perspectives that erode trust are so deeply entrenched in hearts and minds that they make people blind to the need for reconciliation and the beauty of it.

• *Geography*

Many black people believe whites sit comfortably in their homogeneous suburbs and have no clue about the real problems faced by people of color. In the 50s, 60s, and 70s, the demographics in major cities underwent a sweeping change. White flight from cities has a number of causes: the disintegration of downtown areas, blacks moving into predominately white neighborhoods, and banking practices, like redlining and racially restrictive covenants—all of which created conditions of over-crowding and the decline of inner cities. In addition, lenders saw blacks as a credit risk, limiting their housing and business opportunities.

More recently, blacks and Hispanics have been moving into the suburbs, and another round of white flight is oc-curring as whites find other suburbs and exurbs that are all or mostly white. Samuel Kye, a Ph.D. student at Indiana University suggests the move is more about economic factors than intolerance: "There have been some who have argued that white flight isn't actually a response rooted in racial prejudice or attitudes, but instead a natural response to a decline in a neighborhood's median household income or declines in property values that had tended to occur in the past when you had an influx of non-white residents." His study shows that people of color "say their ideal neighborhood is integrated, white people, on average, say predominantly white neighborhoods are desirable."[40]

- *Cultural idolatry*

No, I'm not referring to little statues people worship. Idolatry is putting anyone or anything in the rightful place of God in our lives. Our culture gives us many good things, including values, a particular lifestyle, and a sense of identity, but if we're not careful, we can value our culture more than Christ. When this happens, the trappings of our culture are more important than love, forgiveness, wisdom, kindness, and acceptance.

I grew up in a small town in Georgia, ate country food, listened to country music, talked in a country drawl, went to a country school, and interacted with country people. I

---

40. "White flight didn't disappear—it just moved to the suburbs," Greta Kaul, *Minneapolis Post*, March 21, 2018, *https://www.minnpost.com/politics-policy/2018/03/white-flight-didn-t-disappear-it-just-moved-suburbs/*

didn't carefully compare my culture with others and choose it; it was the only game in town.

When I became a Christian, I was able to take a few steps back and critique my beliefs. I soon realized I was a "country supremacist"—I believed my culture was better than any other.

Virtually all of us start there. I remember talking to a young man who was a second-generation Korean American. I asked him, "What's your biggest challenge fitting in in America?"

He instantly answered, "That's easy. It's getting my parents to let me become more of an American. They believe the Korean culture is far better than the American culture, and they don't want me to switch allegiances. When I'm with them, we go to a Korean church, we eat Korean food, and we shop in stores owned by Koreans. I attended a private Korean school, and my parents live in a Korean neighborhood."

I probed, "Tell me more about that."

His eyes widened. I'd hit a sore spot without knowing it. He said, "If I brought an American girl home to meet my parents, they'd explode. That's inconceivable to them. They would see it as a betrayal of all they hold dear."

Koreans aren't the only ones who might practice cultural idolatry. Whenever we value heritage and habits above people, we're guilty of it.

What do most Americans value supremely? What are our cultural idols? A few years ago, a Christian philosopher identified two pursuits: personal peace and affluence, that is, the right to have a life without hassles and conflicts, and the comfort of having plenty of money to do whatever we want. These passionate goals aren't new. In the second century, Justin Martyr wrote about the way a relationship with Jesus radically changes cultural identity:

> ... we who valued above all things the acquisition of wealth and possessions, now bring what we have into a common stock, and communicate to everyone in need; we who hated and destroyed one another, and on account of their different manners would not live with men of a different tribe, now, since the coming of Christ, live familiarly with them, and pray for our enemies, and endeavor to persuade those who hate us unjustly to live conformably to the good precepts of Christ, to the end that they may become partakers with us of the same joyful hope of a reward from God the ruler of all.[41]

---

41. Justin Martyr, *First Apology*, Chapter XIV.

In the kingdom culture, our passions are turned upside down. Instead of being obsessed with "the acquisition of wealth and possessions," we give generously to those in need. And instead of pursuing peace at all costs by staying away from "men of a different tribe," we move toward them and endure their hostility for the sake of the gospel. Justin Martyr saw that racial reconciliation—and all reconciliation—is only possible when hearts are changed by God's grace.

- *Wounds, long past and recent*

In the body, unhealed wounds are open doors to infection and much worse problems. In the human heart, unhealed wounds are like infections, creating bitterness, making us fragile and overly sensitive, and solidifying our belief that we're victims—and always will be. Self-pity gnaws at our souls, eating away our joy, courage, and love.

We've seen that many whites see themselves as victims of reverse discrimination. Some politicians pick the scabs off these wounds so they stay open and painful. Blacks have many more reasons to have this negative self-perception because they've suffered innumerable injustices for centuries. About 12.5 million Africans were shipped to the New World, mostly to the plantations in the Caribbean and

South America, and almost two million perished on the voyages. The Equal Justice Initiative researched racial terror in the United States and found nearly 6,500 lynchings.[42] Many of these weren't just hangings; they included horrific torture, mutilation, and burning while the person was alive. The goal wasn't just to kill a person but to inflict such prolonged pain that the whole black community was terrified, and therefore, compliant.[43]

In some circles, black anger and bitterness has been fertile soil for reprisals against whites, and it's sometimes met with white guilt and the desire to escape the shame of bigotry ... but not always. As whites feel more like victims, they're voicing their own anger and bitterness, and the divide widens.

• *The presence of evil*

I believe there's more at work in our racial trouble than human selfishness. Spiritual forces enhance the darkness that's already present in sinful hearts. Racism is evil because it demeans people created in the image of God, and it destroys the love we can enjoy with each other. In the same

---

42. "Reconstruction in America," Equal Justice Initiative, *https://eji.org/reports/reconstruction-in-america-overview/*

43. "Lynching in America," Bryan Stevenson, Equal Justice Initiative, *https://eji.org/reports/lynching-in-america/*

letter to the believers in Ephesus, Paul explained that we often fight the wrong battles. Our fight, he said, isn't actually with people, but with deeper, darker spiritual forces: "For our struggle is not against flesh and blood, but against the rulers, against the authorities, against the powers of this dark world and against the spiritual forces of evil in the heavenly realms" (Ephesians 6:12).

It's difficult (and unnecessary) to try to identify the exact source of evil. The factors include what the Bible calls "the flesh," which is the natural human desire to go our own ways and pursue our own purposes; "the world," which is "the flesh writ large" in our culture, including pressures, demands, and institutions that provide a fertile environment for selfishness; and "the devil," the spiritual being and his army who tempt, deceive, and accuse to distract us from God's good path or crush our efforts to follow Him. I don't want to overdramatize the spiritual forces of darkness, but I don't want to minimize them either. When we see men and women—no matter what color—despise people who aren't like them, I'm convinced all three factors are involved. You don't have to believe the Bible to notice evil in the world. It's evident to all of us.

These are at least a few of the bricks that form the wall of racial division in America. There may be others, but these are enough to keep us on edge, believe the worst of each other, and build the wall even higher. But there's another way.

Starting Points

I don't know whether to laugh or cry when I hear well-meaning people announce, "This shooting (or whatever the issue is at the moment) is going to be the breakthrough in race relations in America!" Certainly, a moment can be a starting point, or it can push us one step farther along, but racial division is woven into the fabric of America. It'll take a lot of work and a lot of heart to see substantial change. Let me outline some steps to take some of the bricks off the wall.

• *Humble yourself*

Bob Pierce, the founder of World Vision and Samaritan's Purse, was a deeply compassionate man. He summed up his heart's desire: "Let my heart be broken by the things that break the heart of God." I'm afraid many of us share a deeply flawed view of humility. It's not thinking less of ourselves, berating our character and discounting our talents. It's being so secure that we aren't defensive, too eager to please, or afraid of taking a risk. This exceptionally rare trait gives us the ability to listen instead of insisting on being heard.

Racial tension is always about power—or the lack of it: financial power, political power, and personal power. But God's power only operates when people are humble. The apostle Peter wasn't known for his humble spirit. As the spokesman for the twelve disciples, he was impetuous and self-confident ... until his colossal failure to stand up for Jesus when a servant girl asked if he knew Him. Peter experienced crushing shame, but Jesus graciously forgave him and restored his sense of purpose. In his first letter to believers throughout the Roman Empire, Peter showed that he had learned the most important lesson. He wrote,

> All of you, clothe yourselves with humility toward one another, because,
>
> "God opposes the proud
>   but shows favor to the humble."
>
> Humble yourselves, therefore, under God's mighty hand, that he may lift you up in due time. Cast all your anxiety on him because he cares for you (1 Peter 5:5-7).

Proud people are defensive and defiant, or they may be fragile and demanding, but humble people have enough inner strength to reach out and embrace people who aren't like them and who can't give anything to them. They know how to love.

We can't manufacture a humble heart. It has to be created in us by a genuine experience of God's grace. If we believe our goodness earns points with God, we'll always look down on people we don't consider as good as we are. That's the problem for many people, including many in the church: No matter how many sermons they've heard and songs they've sung, they still think they're better than others.

Grace flourishes when we're broken, when we're shattered by our failure, like Peter was. Jesus didn't look out from heaven and decide, "Those people are pretty good. I'll accept them—but not those others." No, Paul makes it clear in his letter to the Romans that Jesus didn't come to affirm good people; He came to save lost people. We were "powerless," "ungodly," "sinners," and "enemies" of God (Romans 5:6-10). Jesus became vulnerable so we can be secure in His love. He emptied himself so we could be filled with His kindness. He opened His arms wide and was nailed to the cross, so He could open His arms wide to accept us as His own. If this magnificent truth has put down even a tiny root in our hearts, it will revolutionize our lives. We'll be more secure, more honest, and more compassionate—and we'll want to show Jesus' love to people who are heartbroken, defiant, discouraged, and in desperate need of love.

• *Be intentional*

Racial reconciliation (or at least any steps of progress toward it) requires us to be intentional. We have to break the mold of our usual behavior and do whatever it takes to connect with people of other races. We've seen that Jews and Samaritans hated each other. In fact, Jews traveled far out of their way to keep from going through Samaria, but Jesus made a point of going through there. He could have gone around, His disciples undoubtedly expected a respected Jew to go around, and the people of Samaria expected Him to go around, but He didn't.

He and His disciples came to a town called Sychar. At noon a woman came to a well to draw water for the day, but this was very strange. Women came early in the morning. Why didn't she come with the others? Because she was an outcast among outcasts, but Jesus was intentional about connecting with her.

Jesus sent the disciples into town to buy lunch. (One person commented that He sent 12 grown men to buy lunch for 13.) After they left, He didn't wait for her to say anything. He asked, "Will you give me a drink?" She was stunned. It was unheard of—a Jewish man taking initiative to talk to a Samaritan woman! We get to eavesdrop on their conversation. She is at one point eager to listen and receive "living water" and then ashamed to tell the truth about her sex life, but through it all, Jesus assured her of His love. She responded in faith and went into town to tell everyone who would listen about the Savior who cared enough to love her ... even her.

When we started our church, we didn't wait for people of color to come to us. We went into their world. We were intentional about hiring staff who represented the mix of races we believed God wanted in our church. We were intentional about selecting people for our board, because Colleen and I wanted to demonstrate that we could submit to a black leader. We were also intentional about the mix of faces on our stage every Sunday.

When I see a church that has only one color on the stage, I assume they weren't aware of their mistake, and they missed opportunities to reach across racial divides. Or if it was intentional, it's racism, excluding (or at least minimizing) other races on purpose.

Toleration isn't the same as reconciliation, and social niceties aren't the same as genuine love. On a personal level, we need to be intentional about meeting and connecting in meaningful ways with people of other races and cultures. We can make a conscious choice to walk over to a person of a different color to introduce ourselves. Maybe, just maybe, we'll find we have something in common and friendship develops. But even if we have very little in common, we can still be like Jesus and overlook the differences to have a relationship with that person. We might actually learn something new!

Being intentional has many sides. Many years ago in Richmond, Colleen and I were intentional about inviting people to have lunch with us after church. We had many wonderful meals and made a lot of great friends. When Colleen and I moved into our home 20 years ago, about 85 percent of our neighborhood was white. As more minorities moved in, many whites moved out, but we stayed. When we saw a moving van in front of a house, and particularly when we realized a family of color was moving in, we went over to introduce ourselves and welcome them to the neighborhood. We didn't want them to wonder what "those white people" thought about them. From the beginning, we wanted to dispel any hint of suspicion.

To be honest, our decision to stay has probably come at a cost, a financial one. Our home value may not be what it was a few years ago, but that's a price Colleen and I are willing to pay to stay in a mixed-race neighborhood. It's not that blacks, Hispanics, or Asians aren't keeping their yards as nice as the white people—quite often, they're more beautiful—but hard-nosed real estate values don't respect expressions of love.

• *Adopt the kingdom culture*

Jesus told Pilate, "My kingdom is not of this world" (John 18:36). Every moment of every day, we have a choice of where we live: in the culture of the world's values or in Jesus' kingdom culture. The world's culture is all about power, privilege, possessions, and prestige, but Christ's kingdom is the exact opposite: we serve, we give, we love, and we honor others more than ourselves. Christ is our Savior, our example, and our King. We respond to His love by loving Him in return, loving Him more than anything the world promises, and loving the people He loves—which is everybody.

As we change our agendas from an earthly culture to a kingdom culture, we'll see people through a different lens.

Like Jesus with the Samaritan and Paul with the Gentiles, we'll look past surface conditions like the color of skin or national origin, and we'll love without limits. Paul reminded the Colossians: "Here there is no Gentile or Jew, circumcised or uncircumcised, barbarian, Scythian, slave or free, but Christ is all, and is in all" (Colossians 3:11).

How do we know when we're making real progress? It's when we have people of other races into our homes, play with their children, listen to their stories, and connect with their hearts. It may take a while for the walls to come down—ours and theirs—but this is where the nagging problems of racial division in our country begin to heal, loving one person at a time.

Can you say that you have friends from other races who are dear to you? Do you have people like this whom you call at 3:00 in the morning when you're in need or you invite over to celebrate a birthday, anniversary, or any other occasion?

Not long ago, Colleen and I were at our beach house in Florida, and a family of black people—parents and their six kids—had rented a townhouse a few doors down. The row of townhouses was owned mostly by white people. As the black family played on the beach and in the water, I could imagine the conversations in the other townhouses as white people watched them.

Not long ago, a white couple from Mississippi bought a beach house near us. That day as I sat on our porch, I saw this woman walk with her dogs toward the black family. She stopped to talk to them and let the kids play with her dogs. A few minutes later, I saw her walk back to her house. She took them two kayaks and a skimboard. I'm sure this family was surprised, at least for a moment, at this white Southern lady offering all of this when she didn't know them.

Later, I talked to her about what I'd seen. Her name is Bobbie Sue, and she's as country as her name sounds. Her intentional kindness shattered the stereotype of white people from Mississippi. She gave that family a great time in the water, and she took a brick (maybe two) off the wall that separates us.

At another time, Colleen and I were at our home in Florida with another black family renting next door. A couple of the dads and their children were trying to catch fish behind our place, but they weren't having any luck. I walked out and told them what to use for bait, and they thanked me. A little later, when I was riding my bike near a bait store, I felt the Lord tell me to buy the family some bait. When I got back, I gave them two containers of bait. Later that evening, I saw them and asked if they caught any fish. One of the women in the group startled me with her excitement. She told me they had caught over 100 fish that day! She grabbed me by the hand and took me inside and started giving me fish stew, fish casserole, and just about anything you can make with fish! Something happened in that moment between this family and me—it was so beautiful that I'll never forget it. I had the privilege of giving this black family a different experience with white people, and we created an instant and authentic bond. From that moment, we were like family, and boy, did we enjoy some fish!

I often wonder what the world would look like if more people would adopt the kingdom culture and give people an experience of being loved and honored?

Think About It:

Why are simple solutions to race relations so attractive? Why don't they work?

What are some practical ways to lower the level of distrust between races?

How would you define and describe "cultural idolatry"? How do you see it affect people? How about you?

How is the experience of grace essential to develop a humble heart? What can we assume about people who aren't humble?

What is one intentional thing you can do in the next 24 hours to connect with someone of a different race?

chapter 9

Stand Up, Speak Up

A man dies when he refuses to stand up for that which is right. A man dies when he refuses to stand up for justice. A man dies when he refuses to take a stand for that which is true. —Martin Luther King, Jr.

A FRIEND OF MINE who lives in the Deep South has moved up the spectrum toward inclusion, and he has become an advocate of reconciliation, but he has paid a price. He leads a men's group at his church, and when they discussed the demonstrations and fights just after Charlottesville, they noticed that he didn't join them in their outrage at those who were asking for the Confederate monuments to be removed. One of the men asked, "Richard, aren't you angry? Aren't you upset that Antifa has taken over and is inciting violence?"

With every eye on him, Richard responded, "I'm angry, and I'm upset, but not with Antifa. I agree that they're not helping, but I believe the demonstrators have every right to ask that the monuments to Confederate generals be removed. I'm more upset with the white supremacists carrying Nazi emblems and wearing Klan symbols."

Several of the men raised their voices and spoke at the same time: "How can you say that?" "Don't you believe the South had the right to secede?" "Those generals were fine Christian men, unlike the Northern generals!" "You're trying to deny our history and destroy our legacy!"

Richard let them have their say, and then he said, "Let me ask you one question: Do you believe slavery was a moral good or a moral evil?"

One of the men instantly responded, "You have to understand the times. Slavery was accepted, it was normal, and the church defended it. Almost nobody in the South believed it was wrong."

"But do you?" Richard asked again.

The man bristled, "I think it was perfectly acceptable in that time."

The men in the group never saw Richard the same way again. From that day, they believed he was at least mistaken, but more probably, at least a few of them concluded he was a traitor to their sacred heritage. The Lost Cause defense of the South is still alive and well in white churches. Many are still unwilling to peel the layers of justification off the evils of slavery and see it for what it was. And similarly, they're unwilling to take a hard look at discrimination that was institutionalized for a century after the Civil War and the effects that are still with us today. Others are willing to admit slavery was wrong, but they insist, "That's ancient history, and it doesn't have any impact on race relations today."

Sparks

Standing up for truth and justice inevitably creates sparks. Jesus didn't mince words about the cost of following Him: "If anyone comes to me and does not hate father and mother, wife and children, brothers and sisters—yes, even their own life—such a person cannot be my disciple" (Luke 14:26). I don't believe Jesus meant for us to literally hate people. The concept of "hate" in this context is preference. He was saying, "If you value other people's opinions more than Mine, if you live to please them more than Me, if you change your stripes to fit in with people who disagree with you instead of standing up for justice, you belong to the earthly kingdom, not My kingdom."

White apathy and the willingness to justify evil understandably destroy trust and infuriate black people.

I understand because I was one of those white people. Before God opened my eyes to the need for racial reconciliation, I drove by Confederate statues all the time and never gave them a second thought. But when I realized these soldiers fought to protect the ability of Southerners to own human beings for profit, my heart changed. Why in the world would I feel comfortable with celebrations of leaders who killed other Americans over the right to own people? Can anything be less humane? Can anything be less biblical? Is this the past we want to honor? I'm sure I'll get a few emails about this comment, but how would Jewish people in Europe feel about monuments to Hitler or Himmler? They'd be outraged! And they'd be bewildered that anyone would think it was a good idea. Only neo-Nazis defend the brutality and cruelty of Hitler's Germany. Yes, the Holocaust is part of their history, but it's not a treasured history. It's a shameful one.

Not Enough

Clearly, we haven't made as much progress in race relations as many of us thought. We can hope we'll return to calm after the next round of protests over another police killing of a young black man, and we can assume it won't happen in our neighborhoods, but apathy and willful ignorance aren't good enough—especially for those who claim to have been transformed by the sacrificial love of Jesus.

It's not enough for people of color to stand outside the inner circle of society and complain. Oh, they have a lot to complain about, but if all they do is complain, they lose their voice because white people won't listen. And it's not enough for white people to wring their hands and grovel in white guilt. (Let me be clear: White guilt is a better response than white rage, but it's not the same as loving inclusion.)

The recent protests over the death of George Floyd engulfed hundreds of cities and towns throughout the country, and some communities saw riots and looting. People of color and whites of conscience are again calling for change, but too often, blacks perceive supportive whites as "not quite woke"—good intentions aren't the same as genuine understanding and tangible support. Chad Sanders is a black writer who received dozens of texts and emails from his white friends during the news coverage of the recent riots. He observes:

White people are pushing me and others like me aside to alleviate their own guilt and prove that they are different from Officer Derek Chauvin, who killed George Floyd in Minneapolis, and Amy Cooper, who tried to weaponize her whiteness by calling police on Christian Cooper, a bird watcher, in Central Park. Black people are being trampled in the process. Many white people I know are spilling over with guilt and overzealous attempts to offer sympathy. I have been avoiding them as best I can.

Sanders said the offers of sympathy from white friends actually show they don't get it. They don't understand the breadth and depth of the struggle of blacks to live in a white world. He concludes, "As a black man, what I actually feel—constantly—is the fear of death; the fear that when I go for my morning stroll through Central Park or to 7-Eleven for an Arizona Iced Tea, I won't make it back home. ... But the fear doesn't arrive only in the wake of uniquely viral killings of black people such as George Floyd, Breonna Taylor and Trayvon Martin. It's a resting hum under every moment of my life."[44]

Many white people are outraged at the violence and looting that happen in conjunction with legitimate protests. They wonder, *Why would they destroy their own stores and neighborhoods?* Martin Luther King, Jr., gives us the answer, "A riot is the language of the unheard." This observation

---

44 "I Don't Need 'Love' Texts from My White Friends," Chad Sanders, *New York Times*, June 5, 2020, https://www.nytimes.com/2020/06/05/opinion/whites-anti-blackness-protests.html?action=click&module=Opinion&pgtype=Homepage

doesn't condone riots, and it doesn't excuse them, but it helps us understand the incredibly powerful emotions that propel them.

One Up and One Down

Ultimately, it's all about our sense of power. Many white people have a deeply ingrained sense of racial superiority. It's so deep that it's second nature, and they don't even think about it. It's a foundational assumption deep in the recesses of their hearts. Whites have been *one up* in America for 400 years and resent any attempts to replace them in their position of power, which is exactly what many of them believe is happening. They're attracted to the promise to "Make America Great Again" because it promises to restore their position of power and superiority. This, of course, is especially true for older white people who grew up during the time when Jim Crow segregation was gradually replaced with new laws protecting the rights of all people.

In the black community, inferiority is just as deeply ingrained. They've been *one down* for generations. Black parents have to teach their kids how to respond when they're stopped by the police, they have to work harder to get a good education, they often have to have better credit than white people to buy the same house, they're often passed over for promotions, and they have fewer options in virtu-ally every aspect of their lives.[45] They see "Make America Great Again" as putting them back in their place of inferi-ority and compliance.

As we saw in earlier chapters, these assessments aren't guesses or assumptions; they're facts based on incontro-vertible research. We won't make much progress in race relations until the power differential is more balanced. That means the proud need humility, and the oppressed find dignity. Righting these wrongs always makes people feel very uncomfortable, and they react by being defensive or demanding—or both.

When we stand up and speak up for racial reconciliation, we avoid the easy clichés of hate. We don't give blanket ap-provals and condemnations. Instead, we look underneath the inflammatory rhetoric to see what's going on in people's hearts. We move toward angry people of color, so we can understand the depth of their despair. We move toward an-gry white people, so we can grasp the source of their inse-curity. We move toward people who are on the fence to help them find the courage to take a stand for what's right. In

---

45. "On Views of Race and Inequality, Blacks and Whites are Worlds Apart," Pew Research Center, June 27, 2016, *https://www.pewsocialtrends.org/2016/06/27/on-views-of-race-and-inequality-blacks-and-whites-are-worlds-apart/*

all of this, we'll pay a price. If we're white, other whites will believe we've become liberal, and we've denied our heritage. If we're black, other blacks will assume we're not sufficiently militant, and we've become complicit with white power structures. Whenever we stand up, we'll be slapped down. The question is this: Is it worth it?

Grace and Truth

In some circles, standing up for the rights of others is like waving a red flag in front of a bull—it's guaranteed to get a reaction! If you're trying to help a family member or a friend move a notch or two up the spectrum toward inclusion, let me give you some practical advice.

• *Ask questions and listen.*

When someone shoots their verbal gun and we return fire, we're escalating the fight, not seeking understanding. It's amazing how people calm down and engage when we calmly ask, "Would you tell me more about how you came to your convictions? I'd like to understand." Don't jump in to challenge and correct. Just ask questions and listen carefully. A rule of thumb is that if I'm not asking second and third follow-up questions, I'm not listening well enough. Yes, I know I've covered this before, but it bears repeating because it's so important.

- *When you challenge a position, pose it as a relational issue.*

For instance, if you're talking about statues of Confederate soldiers, ask, "How would you feel if you were a black person standing in front of a statue of General Lee, Stonewall Jackson, or Nathan Bedford Forrest?" And perhaps ask, "How do you think I could respond if I were standing in front of one of these statues with a black person, and he asked, 'Do you think it's right to honor men who defended the right to own my great-great-grandparents as slaves?'" Or "When was America great for black people?" And then, "How would you convince them that slogan should be attractive to them?" "Do you remember a time in our history when blacks were treated with respect, when they had equal opportunities, or when they had no complaints about unfairness and injustice? When were they arrested in proportion to their population? When have they had outstanding schools? Tell me about that time." Questions like these are pointed, but they can elicit more empathy than arguing a point and counterpoint.

- *Find common ground.*

If you listen long enough, and if your patience convinces the other person you understand, it's appropriate to say, "Let me give you my point of view. You may not agree with everything I believe, but I think we can agree on some things." Don't rush the process. It's not a 30-minute show that has to have an airtight conclusion by the end. It's not even important that you say everything you want to say. If there's understanding and respect, you can pick it up at a later time and make more progress. And in my experience, changing a deeply held conviction requires many, many conversations and experiences. Be patient, be kind, and realize you're asking the person to overcome years of beliefs and habits. If you begin with what you agree on, you have a much better chance of making real progress toward open and honest conversations.

• *At some point, you're done.*

Some people refuse to even consider another point of view. We all know people like this. They're dogmatic and demanding. They're sure they're right and nothing will make a dent, no matter how skillfully and graciously we communicate with them. At some point, it's foolish to keep coming at them. When you've given it your best shot and you see no opening, it's time to stop trying. Two verses in Proverbs may seem contradictory on the surface, but they actually give us insight about how to respond to obstinate people:

Don't respond to the stupidity of a fool;
you'll only look foolish yourself.

Answer a fool in simple terms
so he doesn't get a swelled head. (Proverbs 26:4-5, MSG)

There are times when we refute a foolish person clearly and precisely, but if we've tried over and over and we've seen no progress, the label of "fool" shifts to us if we keep trying. When we look at the life of Jesus, we see Him actively pursue people like the Samaritan woman He met at the well, the tax collector Zacchaeus, and many others, but He was also willing to let people walk away. The rich young ruler approached Jesus and asked what it took to inherit eternal life. Jesus saw into his heart and addressed the one thing the man wasn't willing to give up: his money. When the man walked away, Jesus didn't chase after him. He respected the man's right to make his choice and live with the consequences. In a similar way, I've talked with obstinate white people and angry people of color, and even though I've tried my best to move them toward reconciliation, I've failed. I patiently asked questions, tried to personalize my perceptions, and listened carefully, but when I pushed back even very gently, they were furious. I soon realized the conversation wasn't going in a good direction. When they walked away, I felt sad—for them, for their families, and for the people they relate to every day—but I didn't badger them with my convictions in an attempt to force them to agree with me.

Not long ago, I had separate conversations with a young mom and her parents. To say the least, they didn't see eye to eye about the political situation in America. The parents told me, "We can't talk to her! She's so unreasonable! I can't imagine why she believes what she believes!" And the young woman's words were almost exactly the same, "I can't talk to them! How can they vote for somebody like that? Why won't they listen to reason?" I advised all three of them to have a cooling off time, and I also told them it's probably not going to be productive for them to talk about politics for a long time.

• *Don't be surprised.*

When I've tried to have meaningful conversations about race relations, more whites have been condescending than obstinate. When I talked to a pastor and shared what we're doing at Victory to bring the races together, he smiled and patted me on the shoulder: "That's wonderful, Dennis. Good for you. I'm so glad you're doing that. I'm sure you're helping a lot of people." It doesn't take a degree in psychology to understand that his words were polite, but he was really blowing me off. He had no intentions of learning anything and doing anything in his church to promote reconciliation. I wish he had looked me in the eye and said, "That's fine for you, but not for me. We're not into that."

I used to be surprised when people's words didn't match their hearts, but I caught on pretty fast. This is a form of paternalism on the scale from inclusion to racism. It's pleasant, and it often prompts generosity to provide for needs, but it's still based on racial superiority.

- *Wait for another chance.*

Over the last 30 years, I've seen some remarkable transformations. I've seen angry, bitter black people find comfort in the love of Jesus and begin to love whites, and I've seen arrogant, prejudiced white people melt in humility and reach out to people of color with remarkable kindness. None of these changes happened in the first conversation. If I'd insisted on instant change, it never would have happened. I would have ruined the opportunity for the Holy Spirit to work deeply—if slowly—in their hearts.

• *Choose who you lose.*

This principle applies to close personal relationships as well as to pastors and their churches. When we take a stand for equality and inclusion, some people in our families and some of our friends won't like it one bit. When we get pushback from them, we have to choose: to cave in and preserve the relationship on their terms, or to hold our ground and risk losing them. If they're family members, we're probably not going to actually lose them, but we'll lose the closeness we wanted. At that point, it isn't an academic exercise any longer. These are people we've treasured, people we trusted, people we thought we understood and we hoped understood us. It's very hard to conclude that our perspectives on race can cause a genuine rift in relationships, but it can.

I've talked with pastors who, especially in light of the politicized nature of evangelicals in recent years, have had to make some painful decisions about the stand they take. White evangelicals are overwhelmingly conservative Republicans, and when the demographics of communities shift and people of color move in and come to the church, pastors often see a mass exodus of whites. Are they willing to lose the white people (who often are the most generous givers) for the sake of the newcomers, or do they move the church to a nearby community that's mostly white?

For a while, pastors in this situation can try to manage both groups of people, but sooner or later, they have to make a decision, hopefully based on biblical values and not cultural and financial expediency. They need to preach the truth of God's Word even if it offends people who aren't comfortable loving their neighbors. Patience is a virtue, but waiting too long to stand up for equality isn't. If pastors refuse to endorse a particular candidate, one group may get upset. Or if they choose to endorse that candidate, the other group is understandably hurt and disappointed. When pastors delay decisions about race, they run the risk of offending everybody. The minorities don't feel welcomed, and the whites realize the pastor isn't as supportive as they thought. In that case, pastors can lose a lot more people.

I told a pastor in this situation, "No matter what you do, people leave churches, but you get to choose who you lose. I preach about tithing, and some people who come to our church feel uncomfortable with my emphasis on it. Am I worried those people will leave? Not too much. The way people handle their money tells me a lot about their hearts for God. If they aren't willing to give generously to the work of God, they aren't going to participate in the life and mission of the church. It's the same with race. If people are uncomfortable with my preaching on racial reconciliation and our church's heart for all people, I'm sure they can find a monochromatic church where they aren't challenged to take down racial walls. If I lose them, I'm okay with that. I'm not okay with watering down the truth of God's grace for every single person, so I can keep a few more people. I'm happy when people come and say, 'Pastor, I'm not where you are, but I'm willing to learn about how to love people of other colors.' Actually, that thrills me! They're on the path, and they want to go farther. It's my great privilege to help them take the next step. I believe God's church includes people of all races, all economic classes, and all political persuasions. We may be very different, but we find common ground at the cross of Jesus."

Jesus didn't follow church growth principles, and He wasn't devoted to building a large following. At the height of His ministry, thousands were following Him. After He fed the five thousand with a boy's sack lunch, He tried to take His disciples on a retreat, but the crowd followed Him. When they caught up with Him, they didn't want Him; they wanted Him to feed them again. In a tense and emotionally escalating confrontation, they demanded bread, but He insisted that they were missing the point. He told them, "I am the bread of life" (John 6:48). They still didn't get it, so Jesus shocked them: "Very truly I tell you, unless you eat the flesh of the Son of Man and drink his blood, you have no life in you." They had no clue what He was talking about. Was He telling them to become cannibals? No, He was insisting that they see Him as the only true source of spiritual nourishment. It wasn't a very popular message. On hearing it, many of his disciples said, "This is a hard teaching. Who can accept it?" And almost the entire crowd of people turned their backs on Jesus and walked away. Jesus didn't beg them to stay, and He didn't even insist that His twelve closest followers stick with Him. He asked them, "You do not want to leave too, do you?" Peter answered for them, "Lord, to whom shall we go? You have the words of eternal life. We have come to believe and to know that you are the Holy One of God" (John 6:48-69).

Why are so few Christians known for their love for people of other races? I think it's simple: They value loaves and fishes more than Jesus, they aren't willing to climb down from their one-up position, and Jesus isn't their true source of spiritual nourishment. When individuals are captured by the love of Jesus, they do what Jesus did: They reach out to the down-and-out and the up-and-comers to love them in Jesus' name. And when churches are captured by the love of Jesus, they become places where racial hurts are healed, the proud become humble, the shamed are treasured, walls of distrust are broken down, and every meeting is a melting pot of races who are committed to understand each other and believe the best of each other.

Jesus was willing to lose everybody so that those who stayed would never wonder what He stood for or the price He was willing to pay for a grace that truly transforms. And if they stayed, they'd be willing to pay the same price.

Actually, we pay a price either way. If we're courageous, we pay a price in the ridicule of those who oppose us and in those who leave us. If we vacillate and equivocate, we pay a price in our hearts because we've caved under pressure, and we fail to point people to the One who was willing to give everything for people who were His enemies.

Which price will you pay?

Think About It:

If you were a young person with parents who resist building bridges with people of color, how would you approach them to help them take steps toward inclusion?

How does it help to personalize questions, so they put people in an imaginary moment with someone they disagree with?

When is it time to walk away? Have you come to that point with someone? What's your next move?

What does it mean to "choose who you lose," individually and as a church?

Describe the price you'll pay for standing up for racial reconciliation, and describe the price you'll pay if you don't.

chapter 10

I Have a Dream

*I have a dream that one day on the red hills of Georgia,
the sons of former slaves and the sons of former slave
owners will be able to sit down together at the table of
brotherhood. ... I have a dream that my four little children
will one day live in a nation where they will not be judged
by the color of their skin but by the content of their
character. I have a dream today.*
—*Martin Luther King, Jr.*

I HAVE THE SAME dream. A few years ago, I gave a
series of messages called "Future Church." I wanted to
look at two dimensions: near and far. What can the people
of God become in our lifetimes, and what is the promise of
what God's people will be in the *palingenesia*, the renewal
of all things described in many places in the Scriptures.

The Shift

I see a dramatic shift in American culture. The younger
generation, those under 40, see things very differently

than older people. At one point, some of John the Baptist's followers asked Jesus why He didn't follow certain rituals the way they and the Pharisees did. He told them a parable they could easily understand:

> No one sews a patch of unshrunk cloth on an old garment, for the patch will pull away from the garment, making the tear worse. Neither do people pour new wine into old wineskins. If they do, the skins will burst; the wine will run out and the wineskins will be ruined. No, they pour new wine into new wineskins, and both are preserved (Matthew 9:16-17).

Jesus was ushering in a new era of kingdom values, kingdom purposes, and kingdom choices. I would imagine few of those reading this book have wineskins in the pantry at home, so let me explain. When wine ferments, it expands. For this reason, new wine needed fresh wineskins that were supple enough to expand with the fermentation. Old wineskins were less elastic, so they couldn't stand the pressure of the fermentation process. The old wineskins represented the Pharisees' teaching and behavior: superiority and exclusion, and comparison and rejection of anyone who didn't measure up to their exacting external standards. But Jesus was bringing the new wine of grace, love, and inclusion. Then as to-day, when love expands a person's heart, the old ways can't hold it! Legalism (earning approval by keeping stated rules) or moralism (earning approval by being good) are the opposite of the free gift of amazing grace. As we've seen, Paul explained it this way, "Therefore, if anyone is in Christ, the new creation has come: The old has gone, the new is here!" (2 Corinthians 5:17)

As I thought about these passages and the future of the church, I wondered, *Am I an old wineskin trying to hold on to the traditional, ineffective ways, or am I a new wineskin, eager to see God ferment His love in my heart and through me to nourish others?* The Pharisees had the same choice, and they fought hard to stay with the old. In fact, they feared and hated the new so much that they killed the One who was bringing it. Today, many white people in the church are saying, "I don't feel comfortable with sitting side by side with people who don't look like me. I don't like these protests. If they'd just settle down and be more responsible, everything would work out well." People of color in the church are saying, "The old ways oppressed people like us. It looks like the best you can do is feel sorry for us, but that's not equality. I AM

A MAN; I AM A WOMAN. I'm somebody. Can't you understand that?"

Many in the younger generation are already there. They get it. They're already reaching out to accept each other. Many of them say, "I don't value people simply based on their race," and they wonder at the entrenched, negative perspectives of their parents and grandparents. I believe the issue of racial justice and equality are at the forefront of generational change in America. If the church doesn't get on board, we're going to lose the generation of young people who see us as soft bigots—but bigots nonetheless.

Young people who have a strong spiritual background are especially disenchanted with what they see as heartless defensiveness in older Christians. They hear the concerns over rioting and looting, and they ask, "Why do you think they're so angry? Can't we address that?" They agree that protest movements sometimes go out of control, but to them, the excessive reaction doesn't completely invalidate the initial motivation for the protest.

When we look at the picture of the future of God's people, we see upheaval, but we also get a glimpse into the unity and love that will someday be true for all who believe. And it certainly appears to me that it will look a lot more like what young people want than what older people are so afraid of.

The Near Future

Things will get a lot worse before they get better. Conflict will be between nations and between spiritual king-doms. Jesus warned, "Nation will rise against nation, and kingdom against kingdom." Christians will hate other Christians, and the haters will find preachers and teachers who affirm and amplify their resentments. Jesus predicted, "At that time many will turn away from the faith and will betray and hate each other, and many false prophets will appear and deceive many people. Because of the increase of wickedness, the love of most will grow cold, but the one who stands firm to the end will be saved" (Matthew 24:7, 10-13). False prophets surface in government, the church, business, the media, and other institutions. Their impact is to divide, not to unify; to accelerate anger and fear, not to inspire trust and hope. Are we seeing any of this today?

After studying the Bible and watching current events for many years, I've concluded that people in the world will continue to be divisive. Their hatred gives them three things they desperately want: an identity as "the ones who have been wronged," a powerful sense of community with others who are full of resentment, and a surge of adrenaline that keeps them on an emotional high. They'll continue to look for candidates who affirm their anger, and they'll support policies that give them an advantage over "those people."

In the middle of the resentment, fear, and hate, a few people will stand up and tell others about the love, forgiveness, and acceptance found only in Jesus. "And this gospel of the kingdom will be preached in the whole world as a testimony to all nations, and then the end will come" (Matthew 24:14). True Christians won't get caught up in the whirlwind of explosive emotions and recriminations. They'll stand up and speak the truth in love to anyone who will listen. False prophets will use the Bible to lead people astray and promote more hostility, but true believers will point people to the transforming grace of God.

Who am I in this story? And who are you? Peter had to be prodded by God to reach out beyond his own race to love others (Acts 10), and he needed a reminder from Paul to prevent him from sliding back into exclusion (Galatians 2), but eventually, he got it. He wrote to a blend of all races: "But you are a chosen generation, a royal priesthood, a holy nation, His own special people, that you may proclaim the praises of Him who called you out of darkness into His marvelous light; who once were not a people but are now the people of God, who had not obtained mercy but now have obtained mercy" (1 Peter 2:9-10, NKJV). When we trust in Jesus as Savior and Lord, we become citizens of God's nation—a holy nation within our earthly nation. Racial resentment, fear, and superiority are part of the darkness, but Jesus has called us "out of darkness into His marvelous light" of love, a love that moves us toward racial reconciliation. A Christian doesn't go with the cultural flow; a Christian goes with the gospel of Jesus, the message of sacrificial love, and a heart out to care for everybody, especially the disadvantaged.

Sadly, very few Christians live this way. When most leave the church after a service on Sunday, their lives are no different from the millions who never went to church. They have the same prejudices, soak up the same caustic news programs, and live with the same fears and bitterness that are in the lives of those who don't know God. Popular author and speaker Beth Moore looks at how some Christian leaders defend racist and divisive policies with harsh rhetoric: "I do not say this lightly or hastily but with fear & trembling after much deliberation. I think we are experiencing a divine reckoning in America. I don't think the reckoning is over our having simply sinned. I think it's over the fact that we have used God & the Bible to do it."[46]

Jesus didn't come to form a political party or institute particular forms of government. He came to change society as born again people learn to love God and love their neighbors—especially those we didn't love before. In our polarized nation, we pigeonhole people as liberal or conservative, Democrat or Republican, and if they're on the other side, we're sure they're either evil or fools ... or both. I've heard conservatives say, "If anyone is a Democrat, he can't be a Christian. No way. The Democrats are anti-God." And I've heard progressives mirror this conclusion: "Republicans aren't for social justice. All they care about is power and profits. That's not the gospel, so they can't be Christians." Can we stop this kind of talk? It's not helpful at all. We can learn from each other, we can listen well enough to understand different perspectives, and then we'll probably moderate our views. No, I'm not saying we'll switch sides, but we'll see the points the other side is making, and we'll have at least some understanding of why they think,

---

46. @BethMooreLPM, Twitter, June 5, 2020

feel, and act the way they do. We won't call them fools, and we won't conclude they're evil. We'll say, "That's a good point. I need to think about that and see how it changes my perspective." I'm always encouraged when I see people arguing about something important and one of them says, "I see your point." Those four words can change everything.

In Christ's kingdom, personal responsibility and social justice are both important, adherence to the law and compassion are not incompatible, and a go-for-it vision for missions can coexist with activism to remedy inequality.

You and I stand at a fork in the road. Will we go down the path of our culture, feeling offended by every slight and reacting as victims in demands and self-pity, or will we follow Jesus into His kingdom, seeing others as more important than ourselves, speaking the truth in a way they can hear it and respond, and reaching out to the "younger brothers" who have run away from God as well as the "older brothers" who are self-righteous and angry that anyone is "cutting in line" in front of them? Will we use social media to pour gas on the fires of distrust and resentment, or will we use every means of communication to spread the wisdom, love, and peace God has already poured into our hearts. Will we value only people who look like us, cook like us, shop like us, and celebrate like us, or will we move into the lives of all people to let them know that Jesus loves them? Will our churches be monochromatic, or will they be multicolored and multicultural like they were in the first century and will be again someday?

And Someday

Today, we struggle to find ways to reconcile people of different races and nations, but someday, color and race will make no more difference than the shape of someone's ears. We often look to John's prophecies in Revelation to see "the end of the story," but there are many other pictures of that glorious time. Isaiah lived about seven centuries before Christ, and his vision of our ultimate end is expansive and inclusive. There will come a day, he promises, when evil is vanquished and Jesus reigns without rival. That day, people from all nations will come to Him bringing the finest of their industry and farming. They'll bring strong young camels from Midian, Ephah, and Sheba. They'll bring gold and frankincense and the finest sheep from lands near and far. Ships will sail from distant lands with the most beautiful gold and silver. People who weren't part of the Jewish kingdoms will be full partners in building the city of God, and speaking to the new city ...

Your gates shall be open continually;
  day and night they shall not be shut,
that people may bring to you the wealth of the nations,
  with their kings led in procession.

What is the motivation for such a joyful expression of gratitude? The people from the nations give "for the name of the Lord your God, and for the Holy One of Israel, because he has made you beautiful." Unfettered security, love, and honor will take the shackles off our hearts and free us to be the people God created us to be—completely, totally, and wonderfully. And we'll love each other:

Violence shall no more be heard in your land,
  devastation or destruction within your borders;
you shall call your walls Salvation,
  and your gates Praise. (Isaiah 60:5-7, 9, 11, 18, ESV)

The new heavens and new earth won't be segregated, and there won't be any resentment among the races. All the people there will be treasured, all will be considered beautiful, and all will be God's delight. The process of Christian growth is bringing the wonders of the future into the circumstances of today. When we look at what will be, we want to experience as much as possible today. Faith comforts, but faith also compels. It's not always comfortable or easy to trust God to accomplish His purposes on earth as they are in heaven, but that's our role as His beloved children.

Do This, at Least

What can one person do to right the wrongs of racial injustice? Well, it's not nothing! We can do more than throw up our hands and complain that it's hopeless, that the system is rigged against us, and that we have no power. We do have power—the power to think, pray, and act.

When we're with people who are making racially insensitive statements, we can speak up, not with harsh condemnation, but with understanding. We can say, "I wonder what's led you to think that way." After more interaction, we can add, "I used to believe that, but not anymore." And then we can tell our story of a changed heart.

We can take a hard look at what comes into our minds and hearts. What news feeds do we read, watch, and listen to? What's their angle? (They all have an angle.) Which one is the most insightful and least emotionally explosive? And, we can make some changes in our choice of sources so we can see the other side of any argument.

We can give our time, expertise, and finances to help the disadvantaged, who are disproportionately people of color. Virtually every community has fine organizations that use volunteers to make a difference. And we can support our church's involvement in social justice and caring for the poor. If the church doesn't have an effort like this, we can start one.

We can talk to our families and friends about what we're learning about racial reconciliation. Our kids will probably be thrilled (and maybe shocked), and our friends may be shocked (but not too thrilled). Read good books on the subject, listen to podcasts, and keep feeding your soul with the gospel of grace.

We can develop true friendships with people of other races. This, I believe, is the most important point in this book. None of the principles and statistics will make a dent if we keep people at arm's length. I've talked to a number of people who have told me that the turning point for them happened when a neighbor moved next door or a new person was hired at their company, and they became friends. Suddenly or over time, negative presuppositions faded, respect grew, and true friendship changed the person's view of other races.

You, Even You

It's easy to feed our souls with resentment. The news and social media are designed to grab our attention with sights, sounds, and words that tap into our fears. Reacting in anger satisfies for a moment—in fact, it feels so right!—but it poisons our hearts and takes us farther from God's path. We need courage, we need commitment, we need encouragement, but most of all, we need to experience the love of Jesus so deep in our hearts that He can change us from the inside out.

Jesus didn't make assumptions about people who were very religious. He was glad to meet with Nicodemus, even though the Pharisee was afraid to be seen with Him, so he asked if they could meet at night. Everywhere Jesus went, religious leaders showed up to try to ask questions He couldn't answer so He'd look foolish or to accuse Him of being ungodly because He healed people on days they were sure He shouldn't. They were respected (and even feared) in the community, but they didn't scare Jesus. He spoke the truth to them just as He spoke the truth to prostitutes, hated tax collectors, the blind, the crippled, the lepers, and the sick.

I've written some hard things in this book. I've said that if a person doesn't love, it's a sign he or she may not even be a Christian—no matter what title is held in a church, how regularly the person attends, or how much money is given. I'm not trying to be harsh or overly dramatic; I'm just trying to be honest with you like Jesus was honest with religious people in His day. It's possible to be very religious and miss the heart of God. It's possible to know the Bible inside and out but be blind to the message of grace. It's possible to be a leader in a church and not have a vital relationship with Jesus.

And of course, there are others who may have read to the end of the book who are sure they don't know God. They've read this far because they're curious. They may be white, or they may be people of color, but now they realize they simply can't love the way Jesus loves unless something changes deep in their souls.

If you've been religious and involved in church, but you've failed to love, let me suggest making this prayer your own:

Lord Jesus, I've missed Your heart. I don't know how it happened, but it did. Forgive me for going through the motions for so long without being touched by Your love, forgiveness, and grace. I want to experience Your love so much that it overflows into the lives of others—especially those who aren't like me. Humble me, so I don't look down on anyone. Stop my tongue and my fingers when I'm tempted to join the culture's caustic chorus of self-pity and resentment. Strengthen me, so I'll stand against injustice toward anyone. Bring people into my path, so I can learn to love them like You love them.

If you haven't been religious, but you sense your need for a Savior, make this your prayer:

Jesus, I realize how much I need You. I've gone my own way, and I'm empty. I repent for my sins, and I ask You to forgive me. Thank You for dying in my place to pay the penalty for my sins. I want to know You and follow You. Fill me with Your love, and give me the courage to love people I've considered unlovely. When I open the Bible, speak to me. When I spend time with Christians, use them to help me grow in my faith. I belong to You.

And all of us can pray:

Jesus, You loved those who hated You. You had compassion for those who were lost, who were despised, who were overlooked, who were hurting, and who had run from You. Break my heart with the things that break Yours—apathy, injustice, superiority, and all kinds of mistreatment. Give me courage and clear steps I can take to right the wrongs around me. Give me real friends from other races.

No matter what, don't give up. Our country has been dealing with racism for four centuries. We've defended it, fought over it, despised it, and ignored it, but it's still with us. Keep moving toward people. Do what you can. Your motivation and ability to love "those people" isn't a political decision. It comes because you're convinced of your poverty and wealth—not financial but spiritual. You were a hopeless, helpless sinner, completely devoid of any way to twist God's arm to make Him care for you, but in His matchless love, Jesus stood in your place and suffered, so you could have the untold riches of His grace. You had nothing, but now you inherit everything! Now you can give your heart with incredible generosity to those God puts in your path. Every day is an opportunity to pay it forward. Do it today.

Think About It:

Do you agree or disagree with the statement that we're running the risk of losing the younger generation over issues like racial injustice? Explain your answer.

Jesus predicted things would get worse before they get better. How have you seen resentment give people three things they desperately want: an identity as "the ones who have been wronged," a powerful sense of community with others who are full of resentment, and a surge of adrenaline that keeps them on an emotional high?

How does the wonder of what will happen when Jesus returns affect how we treat people today?

What is one thing you're committed to change in your heart, your perspective, and your attitude toward people of other races?

Which prayer did you pray? How do you think God will answer it?

About the Author

Dennis Rouse is the founding pastor of Victory Church that began in 1990. Over his 30 years as pastor, he and his wife Colleen have helped build one of the most multicultural churches in the world with 142 different nationalities and around 20,000 members. Dennis is also the author of "10" addressing the qualities that move you from a believer to a disciple of Christ. Dennis and Colleen have been married since 1983 and are now in their second phase of life taking the messages they've ministered for years outside the church to help expand the Kingdom of God throughout the world. Their vision includes four major messages: to help churches Build Strong Families, Transform their community, Reconcile cultures, and Reach the world with the gospel of Jesus Christ.

CLAIM YOUR FREE
ANNUAL SUBSCRIPTION

AT AVAILJOURNAL.COM
($59 VALUE)

AVAIL The Journal

ΛVΛIL +

TRY FOR 30 DAYS *AND RECEIVE*
THE SEQUENCE TO SUCCESS
BUNDLE FREE

$79 VALUE

+ BOOK
+ STUDY GUIDE
+ ONLINE COURSE
+ LIVE CLASS
+ MORE

The Art *of* Leadership

This isn't just another leadership collective...this is the next level of networking, resources, and empowerment designed specifically for leaders like you.

Whether you're an innovator in ministry, business, or your community, **AVAIL +** is designed to take you to your next level. Each one of us needs connection. Each one of us needs practical advice. Each one of us needs inspiration. **AVAIL +** is all about equipping you, so that you can turn around and equip those you lead.

AvailLeadership.org/chand

AVAIL LEADERSHIP PODCAST

WITH VIRGIL SIERRA

FOLLOW THE LEADER

STAY CONNECTED

f facebook.com/AvailLeads/   @availleadership   AVAIL